THINKLOVE LEADERSHIP

THINKLOVE LEADERSHIP

A GUIDEBOOK TO ACTIVATE YOUR TRUE POWER

Kelly Tomblin

Kathleen T. Sullivan

Palmetto Publishing Group
Charleston, SC

ThinkLove Leadership: A Guidebook To Activate Your True Power

Photographs by Kathleen T. Sullivan, Soul Images
www.soulimages.com

First Edition

Printed in the United States

ISBN-13: 978-1-64111-372-4
ISBN-10: 1-64111-372-3

ACKNOWLEDGMENTS

Our heartfelt thanks to our friend and colleague, Beverly Good. Without her guidance and persistence, this guidebook would not have been completed. She pushed us and stayed with us throughout its creation and our twenty-five years together. She may stand in the background, but she is always standing—for us, for those in need, and for the world.

Kelly: I owe a deep gratitude to my family of origin—especially my mom and dad, who told me over and over again that my circumstances did not define me. Their love has been by my side every day. To the family I chose—Steve, George, and Harrison—thank you for coming with me wherever I roamed and for not making me feel guilty every day for doing this work. You all have taught me what love looks like in action.

Kathleen: I am very grateful for the love and support of my siblings, Terri, Eileen, Marybeth and Michael throughout the years. Especially to my sister, Terri, for always providing a "home" for me to come back to. Although no longer with us, my mother's authenticity and my father's perseverance will always be my THINKLOVE light. Finally, to my "soul tribe" of amazing women—thank you for blessing me with your loving sisterhood, wisdom, and guidance along my journey.

We both stand in honor of the experience we had at Jamaica Public Service and we thank the leaders of that company and the people of Jamaica for teaching us what ThinkLove can mean to the world.

A final special thank you to the Omega Institute for Holistic Studies for being a bright light to both of us for more than twenty years. Their principles have guided us on our path to mindfulness and purpose, and we are honored to help carry out their mission.

TABLE OF CONTENTS

"*Personal transformation can and does have global effects. As we go, so goes the world, for the world is us. The revolution that will save the world is ultimately a personal one.*" *Marianne Williamson*

The Purpose of this Guidebook

More than half a century ago, Dr. Martin Luther King Jr. famously said, "Power without love is reckless and abusive, and love without power is sentimental and anemic." Since that time, several leadership advocates have echoed that message. Patrick Lencioni framed it for the workplace using the terms healthy and smart. Brené Brown names the balancing act "strong back/open heart." Those and others like them emphasize that true power results in both effectiveness and engagement, and depends on the balance of the masculine and feminine perspectives in the work place. Leadership characteristics exemplifying that balance are now written into performance reviews and documented in leadership manuals. Despite these acknowledgements, however, we continue to struggle to produce a leadership standard that meets that balanced mandate.

A formidable roadblock to creating a new leadership standard appears to be our interpretation of the rules of "power" and how we continue to see it portrayed in the world. Specifically, the usual depiction of a "knowing all, fearing nothing, lording over" confirms our subconscious programming about power with an inconsistent masculine/feminine balance. Accordingly, before we can have a new norm of leadership and a more enlightened demonstration of it, we must expose the implicit beliefs within the word "power" and the many ways we cling to the old ideas and behaviors related to it.

In our research, we have discovered that many of us confuse the word "power" with the word "force" which results in a skewed interpretation of power. In his book *Power vs. Force*, Dr. David Hawkins highlights the difference between the two concepts: "Force is self-interested, divisive, ego-driven and produces a win-lose dichotomy. True power is community focused, unites, mission-driven and produces a win-win objective. True power is total and complete in and of itself and requires nothing from outside of itself. It makes no demands; it has no needs. (Hawkins, 2002). This is not how we currently think of power or see it expressed.

Given that many of us consciously accept the power/force distinction, and given our basic intellectual understanding of "good" leadership traits, why do we still see so much evidence that toxicity and mediocrity are prevalent in leadership? Why do we continue to hear the stories in the press and continue to participate in the movements in the streets about the abuse of power? At the same time, why do we read consistently about the failure to meet our organizational objectives? What is preventing a true leadership revolution? More specifically, why are well-intentioned and educated leaders unable to create the world they want in the workplace even though they lead it?

After many years of studying and participating in leadership, we believe this cognitive dissonance is the result of an inability to override our current mental model of leadership and reset our subconscious programming about what leaders do. In addition, once the reprogramming has been accomplished, there is hesitancy to have the courage to inject the new mental model into the culture.

Our analysis of the actual day-to-day activities of leaders has underscored that one of the most significant challenges to overriding current subconscious models and developing intentional courage is the busyness of leaders. There is simply no time for studying our leadership, and no project plan has been developed to address it. Many leaders tell us their minds are cluttered with information and they devote most of their time to thinking about the past, the future, and the current year's objectives. The ability to be fully present, aware, and focused (mindful) in the moment without being distracted by external noise is rare. Although "mindfulness" has found its way into mainstream language, the action of its practice has not permeated workplace norms.

How, then, do we embed the mindfulness required to overcome these obstacles and the years of subtle implicit teaching about the priorities and behaviors of leadership to activate our true power? We believe it can only be achieved through a committed practice that is supported and incorporated within the psyche of the leader—a practice that can inject a new common language and provide a systematic study of the leader's beliefs and practices of leadership.

This guidebook is designed to provide that study, practice, and language. Beginning with a "ThinkLove" model designed to balance the various aspects of leadership, this guidebook supports the new model by providing one hundred reflections to help you explore your current personal wisdom and perspectives about leadership. Embedded in those reflections are the latest thinking on leadership topics, but the overriding objective of this guidebook is to provide you with a platform for your own unique and consistent leadership exploration. Encouraging a continuous circle of learning, the contents have been designed to allow you to choose the sections that most resonate with you and your situation. Ultimately, we believe this is the only way to activate your own authentic True Power.

Further, we provide you with the space to note and acknowledge your current beliefs and your intention for the future. Since writing or journaling has been shown to enhance mental clarity and improve learning, we strongly encourage you to write down your answers to the questions as part of your practice.

Finally, for the greatest impact we urge you to begin now—right now—and commit to one hundred days. Books are often bought and shelved and, as a result, never lead to a sustainable change in the fabric of our minds. Starting now and making a hundred-day commitment will ensure that this process leads to a meaningful and life-changing moment for you.

Certainly, there has never been more at stake, and the time has never been more urgent for all of us to activate our True Power. Individual well-being and potential, the strength of our communities, the success of our companies, and the sustainability of our world will be determined by our willingness to step up and step into this pivotal time in our history and do the messy, courageous, sacred work of leadership.

A New Model of Leadership: THINKLOVE

The topic of leadership has been studied and written about for decades. In fact, if you search "leadership" on Amazon today, you will find more than 200,000 results. In line with that ubiquity, we have read many of those books and have been exposed to, worked with, and evaluated many models of leadership. While we have found value in most of them and their numerous insights and acknowledge that many of them have been written by skilled and thoughtful authors, we are faced with the fact that there continues to be a great dissatisfaction with the demonstration of leadership.

After studying and evaluating this dissonance, more than thirty years, we have come to the overall conclusion that while there are many different paths to understanding powerful, sustainable leadership, they key to effective demonstration lies in developing a practice of leadership that combines knowledge with individual wisdom. In addition, as we outlined the general characteristics that have been shown to lead to the type of leadership that fundamentally changes the expression and effectiveness of that power, we could not find a general model that incorporated what we have lived and learned. Accordingly, we have offered a new leadership model that touches the core of what we have witnessed, while at the same time offering enough flexibility within the model for leaders to express the essence of their unique leadership authentically. We have labeled this model "ThinkLove." We claim no greater authority on leadership principles with its use, but we believe it provides the missing intimate interaction and integration with those various principles, using your own voice as the ultimate guide.

Undeniably, most institutions, especially those in the corporate domain, were founded by men, and revered the intellectual while discarding the emotional aspects of leadership. This viewpoint was dominant in politics, media, arts, religious organizations, and virtually anytime groups gathered together. While the intellect is valuable and needed, we hold that the intellectual/emotional imbalance and the mind/heart severance has led us to the type of leadership we see predominantly in the world today. In that spirit, we have sought to combine the highest form of the mind and the heart in the "THINK LOVE" acronym we use for the model. To support the ThinkLove concept, we have populated the model with characteristics that we believe to be the core components of True Power: True Self, Trust, Higher Purpose, Integration, Navigation, Knowledge, Listening, Optimism, Vulnerability, and Energy. While not an exhaustive list, we believe these words can lead to rich conversation about leadership and how it looks in its finest hour.

We accept that many other characteristics could apply to the THINKLOVE acronym that we use for our discussion, and that related concepts are included in each letter. For instance, for the "V" in love, we struggled with whether "Vulnerability" or "Voice" was the key component. Ultimately, we felt that in most environments, voice could be encompassed more completely in vulnerability rather than the other way around. We understand that other readers may choose differently, and we welcome your own use of the model in any way that captures your circumstance. With that in mind and with the acknowledgement that the ten components of THINKLOVE do intertwine and often seep into one another, we offer our definitions for these words while encouraging you to regard them as a platform upon which to explore your own articulation of this model as you work with and through it.

We do not intend for this to be a stagnant model. Our hope is that it remains open and morphs according to the culture of the individual or group using it, knowing that your inner wisdom will ultimately lead you to expand on the model and its components as you deem appropriate. We hold that Leadership is always an evolving, living adventure.

The THINKLOVE Model

True Self

Discovering True Self requires the courage to explore who you really are without the limiting beliefs of who you should be. It takes you into an honest conversation about your true values, your most sincere beliefs, your deepest fears, your protective masks, and your future aspirations. In the midst of this exploration, your authentic voice will emerge and help you resist the temptation to imitate, fit in, or stand out. This inner voice will prevent you from puffing up or shrinking. This brave exploration will lead you to embrace your own unique story, what you truly care about, what you are hungry for, what you are innately great at, and what barriers keep you from expressing the highest version of yourself. To reach this continual understanding of self requires practices that embed the inquiry into the fabric of your life and help you discern your voice over the myriad noises that form and target our conscious and unconscious. These supportive practices can include leadership assessments, journaling, meditation, 360 reviews—and, of course, this guidebook.

The True Self knows that the mind and the heart are both present within, and it seeks to express them in balance. It tempers the ego and seeks to be grounded and centered. Most important, our commitment to discovering and embodying the True Self includes the promise to make room for others to do the same and supports a culture of diversity and inclusion. We hold that revealing True Self is a lifelong adventure and the foundation and center for redefining power. Listening to the True Self results in an authentic lifetime legacy. .

Trust

One of the most touted qualities of a successful leader, trust serves as the foundation of all relationships. Since we hold that all work is done through relationships, the focus on trust-building will result in both efficiency and effectiveness. A strong trust environment requires us to manage conflict and hold others accountable, while at the same time demonstrating a deep care and concern for our employees. Many authors have addressed trust—from Miguel Ruiz's "being impeccable with your word" in *The Four Agreements* to Stephen Covey's "character and competence" in *The Speed of Trust*, and Patrick Lencioni's "trust foundation" in *The Five Dysfunctions of a Team*. In addition, many organization evaluations include an assessment of the level of trust. Notwithstanding this ubiquity, we felt it was important to acknowledge the prominent place of trust in the authentic leadership journey. We include within our trust discussion the trust of self, the trust of others, and being trustworthy...which encompasses the ability to know yourself and others. We assess trust through three lenses: character, caring, and competence. For instance, in action, are you impeccable with your word? Do you speak truthfully and with good purpose? Do you show you care through visible actions? Do you demonstrate skill and expertise in your domain? These actions help create the psychological safety needed for true leadership conversations that draw out the best of our human family.

Higher Purpose

We believe the human spirit seeks to bring purpose and meaning to life. While some reject the notion that the world of work plays a role in the higher purpose arena, we acknowledge the truth that much of our lives are spent at work, and our purpose should be displayed there. We proffer that conscious leaders have a power to help redefine the concept of higher purpose and to drive a connection to work that goes beyond the obvious responsibilities. They help articulate the value and meaning behind the work activity, and in doing so, they elevate the respect and value of the employee accomplishing the task. To embed a higher purpose, we articulate the "why" of work and reframe the depiction of hard work. Rather than portraying hard work as heavy or burdensome with a sole focus on the mechanical or tactical responsibilities, we hold the efforts we deliver at work should feel "worth it"—driven by a greater impetus and included in a conversation about the positive impact those contributions will have on customers and communities. Higher purpose conversations should be present in vision/mission/values discussions, and leaders who handle power differently use stories to bring the strategy related to the mission alive. Higher purpose will require us to be comfortable with ambiguity and to consider revolution when all else has failed. The heart of the higher purpose pursuit is the well-known Mark Twain quote, "The two most important days of your life are the day you were born and the day you found out why."

Integration

The concept of integration relates to our ability to unify our internal self and unify with the world around us. Internally, it begins with integrating the various aspects of who we are, including a balance of masculine and feminine traits and energy. It incorporates our compassion and vulnerability, as well as our decisiveness and action-orientation. It seeks to unite our physical, mental, emotional, and spiritual selves. Externally, integration involves bringing people together, breaking down silos and hierarchy, and combining disparate parts of an organization to create one unified entity with a culture of equality. Leaders who integrate understand the power of connection and they work to create a sense of true unity. Integration is not limited to workplace interactions; it extends to ways of being in the world. Integration abhors segregation. A culture of integration, however, requires more than diversity programs. It demands the skill to thwart "island" and "divisive" mentality, and recognizes that leadership and knowledge live throughout the organization. Transformational leaders help weave an employee tapestry that is greater than its parts and reduces the isolation and separateness that is often felt in the workplace.

Navigation

The skill of navigation allows a leader to help create a roadmap that takes the group or organization to their desired outcomes. It allows the leader to be captain of the ship, but not the dictator. These leaders study and understand the external and internal forces driving the company's direction, and they synthesize and communicate this information in meaningful ways to those they lead. To be able to navigate effectively, the leader must be able to inspire the people throughout the journey and describe the destination in a way that draws those they lead to be personally invested in the movement to that place. These leaders do not let people "wander in the desert," and they model being "at cause" rather than "at effect"— meaning, they create circumstances rather than react to them. Navigators help direct the organization in its pursuit of operational excellence and growth, and they steer decisively in times of chaos and confusion. They are change masters who know how to alter course while protecting the underlying mission. They are not afraid to make difficult decisions in defense of that mission. In summary, navigators communicate where the organization is going and how it will get there, and all along the way reminding us of "why" we are going.

Knowledge

Our interpretation of Knowledge includes both the intellectual and the intuitive. In pursuit of intellectual knowledge, leaders are eager to learn and are committed to building knowledge in a variety of domains, including finance, operations, technology, etc. They present evidence that they are serious about that commitment. They devote scheduled time to building both industry and company knowledge, and they approach this inquiry with curiosity and sincere interest. They accept that Knowledge comes from many sources and unlikely places—from a variety of employees and a number of experiences. Most important, they are also students of leadership as a profession, and they invest time and resources into building their competence as a leader.

Regarding intuitive knowledge, well-rounded leaders embed practices that allow them to hear their own inner wisdom, and they use their intuition as a trusted guide. Self-knowledge plays an important role in their intuition and their leadership delivery. They work to combine all knowledge and knowingness in a way that informs holistic and creative decision-making.

Listening

We use a broad interpretation of listening to include hearing ourselves, hearing one another, and hearing the world at large. Following Mark Nepo's *Seven Thousand Ways to Listen*, we hold that listening is sacred and it beckons us to a deeper knowing and understanding of ourselves and others. We believe that the traditional concept of listening is the foundation for human connection, and it requires respect, presence, self-discipline, commitment, and practice. Listening goes beyond the intellectual, and acknowledges cues that are revealed throughout and even before the interaction. The ability to listen helps the leader know how to speak to drive organizational focus and manage performance.

Listening allows us to more intimately know the strengths and weaknesses of others, and it provides data to help us determine progress both in their development and in our own. Leaders who ignite true power seek counsel and understand when to listen rather than speak. They know that listening forms the foundation for their leadership language.

Effective leaders welcome feedback about their blind spots and they help create a culture where being listened to is expected.

When leaders listen to their people and to the world, they leverage all human, physical, and financial assets synergistically. They listen with their whole selves to what is being said and what is not being said; they incorporate an understanding of the impacts of character, culture, and society. They can maximize moments by being completely present—skillfully resisting the temptation to continuously multi-task and reject the now. They honor the role of the figurative or literal "talking stick," and they grant it freely.

Optimism

We hold that optimism is the expression of a belief in possibility, breakthrough, and potential. It is rooted in the conviction that we can move trajectory and circumstances, and design desired outcomes. Optimism injects an energy of positivity, curiosity, and imagination that encourages employees to believe in their individual power to create and manage their futures. Optimism inspires bigger dreams and the action to support those dreams which, in turn, facilitates a productive mood and a positive morale.

Optimism fuels hope and supports resilience. At the same time, optimistic leaders do not ignore reality as part of true optimism—quite the contrary, they articulate hard facts and possible outcomes. However, they believe in the power of declarations, and they know that there are always opportunities to be seized in even the most challenging of times. They reject the fear that limits action and possibilities, and focus on the desired outcome. Most of all, optimistic leaders bring a sense of humor and playfulness to work. They take their work seriously, but never themselves.

Vulnerability

Vulnerability is a precursor to courageous leadership. Contrary to popular thought, vulnerability is not a weakness, even though we have been taught in subtle ways that it is. In fact, we only use the term when there is danger, such as cybersecurity vulnerability, financial vulnerability, and social and economic vulnerability. Consequently, we need to reframe our idea of vulnerability if we are to gain its benefits.

Brené Brown has spent more than twenty years researching vulnerability, and her Ted Talk on this subject has been viewed by more than thirty-seven million people to date. In that talk and in her research, she emphasizes that vulnerability is the birthplace of creativity and innovation and the foundation of all change management. Leaders who are comfortable with being vulnerable lead creativity, innovation, and change more expertly by allowing a "fail fast, ask questions, admit your wrong, and express confusion" culture. In those cultures, our willingness to be seen—truly seen—sets the tone for authenticity throughout the organization. These organizations recognize that without vulnerability there is no growth, there is no learning, there is no trust. All conversations that matter require vulnerability. It takes courage to say, "I don't know," "I'm sorry," "You hurt my feelings," "It was my fault, "I need help", "I love you", etc., so they often go unsaid.

The resolve to be vulnerable is based on the acknowledgment that we all have been shaken or scared, and that by leaning into our ability to experience the vast range of human emotions we will free others to do the same. As we tell our story, we open the connection and intimacy that is required to deliver extraordinary results.

Energy

The focus on energy starts with the commitment to be self-aware about our personal state of energy and to determine what impacts it, both positively and negatively. Managing our energy incorporates the understanding that energy comes from physical, mental, and emotional health, and that our personal energy significantly impacts those we lead. It includes the promise we make to ourselves to maintain physical health, to reduce energetic blocks, and eliminate the toxicity in our lives. Being mindful with our energy directs us to what type of energy is needed for a particular situation. For instance, some moments may call for our warrior energy to emerge, and some may require that we use our voice in a subtler way.

Healthy leaders do not underestimate the overriding influence of workplace energy. They are moved by the truth that organizations can be the most toxic places on earth or can provide a place of growth and healing. They view energy management as part of their leadership promise. Skill in this arena also includes the awareness of where to place our energy personally and organizationally—whether on the small stuff, attracting talent, or eliminating bureaucracy, for example. Leaders who are intentional about their use of energy are more productive and effective.

The energy of an energetic leader is contagious, and it ultimately ignites engagement at work. Leaders who use their energy to "walk the talk and talk the walk" with enthusiasm know that the path to true power is less treacherous when it is fueled with an internal, sustainable, healthy fire.

Summary

This model and the words and definitions incorporated in it are provided to help give language to a renewed idea of leadership that is productive and uplifting. It is our hope that together they will provide a framework for your thinking as you move through the reflections and embed a mindfulness practice into your leadership. Our goal was to make the definitions broad enough to resonate with many different types of leaders and various leadership situations. Strict adherence to the model, however, is not required for your leadership evolution. Again, this process is uniquely your own. Embrace what speaks to you and move through the rest. Your voice is the ultimate guide.

Building the
ThinkLove Practice

To assimilate the concept of the ThinkLove model into your daily leadership practice, we have provided one hundred leadership reflections that incorporate various new thought leadership topics. To use the reflections most effectively, we suggest you start from Reflection 1 and move sequentially through to Reflection 100. We also suggest you read one reflection a day to build momentum and focus. However, a "day" can be interpreted any way you choose, and if moving through the reflections sequentially doesn't work for you, choose your own path using the index provided or following your own intuition. If you are drawn to a particular component of the THINKLOVE matrix, feel free, of course, to start there.

The reflections are supported with questions that require your personal answers. We urge you to use this guidebook or a separate journal to record your answers to the questions posed and to capture any other thoughts you have. Research has proven that reflection and writing things down results in greater learning and behavioral change. With reflective thought, we examine our core beliefs and underlying assumptions, and create an opening for new thinking.

We typically provide about five questions for your contemplation. If any of them do not speak or make sense to you, we encourage you to respond to those that do. We intend for these reflections to apply to various leadership situations. We have used language that may be more applicable to the corporate world, but we have taken that approach for simplicity and we encourage you to interpret the language broadly.

Our greatest hope is that this guidebook establishes a practice for your own unique leadership. Our framework is meant to be flexible and accommodating, recognizing that true power comes from being your true self, charting your own way, and allowing others to do the same.

To help you move through this powerful learning process, we have included a circle of learning cycle that is depicted in a "Mindfulness Map." This Map shows how each activity builds on the next, and ultimately results in continuous growth.

Mindfulness Map

BUILD
leadership knowledge

CREATE
a mindful practice

REFLECT
on your effectiveness

THINKLOVE LEADERSHIP

ASSIMILATE
THINKLOVE concepts

PRACTICE
leadership in your world of work

DISCERN
what speaks to you

"Mindfulness means paying attention in a particular way; on purpose, in the present moment, and nonjudgmentally to the unfolding of experience moment by moment." Jon Kabat Zinn

Reflection Index

Knowledge

Listening

Optimism

Vulnerability

Energy

One Hundred
Leadership Reflections

Reflection #1:
Journey to Self

You have chosen or have been given this guidebook because you are feeling—consciously or subconsciously—an urge for greater depth in your personal leadership, and you are willing to explore an expanded idea of what it means to be a leader. Whether you lead a team, a church, a family, or a large organization, there has never been a more urgent time for this willingness to redefine leadership and power. Clearly the world is demanding for power to express itself differently. Each of us has an opportunity and a role to play in answering that call, regardless of our title or position.

Throughout the next one hundred days, we will engage in that inquiry about how to be a leader who is more powerful, more impactful, and more meaningful—a leader who leads in a way that destroys the notion of hierarchy, control, and limitations, and embraces the truth of unity, authenticity, and a new way of being. The actual time commitment to read the reflections is brief. Accordingly, we urge you to reflect and write and carry them with you throughout the day to allow them to seep into you more deeply.

We hold that the inquiry and the center of all leadership both begin with a deeper exploration of self—the willingness to look at "you" with an honesty that is raw and courageous. We believe leadership demands intimate self-knowledge—the ability to step both inside and outside of yourself, to truly see who you are. This self-knowledge requires a deep commitment for and a practice to foster self-awareness that continues over time as we evolve and change.

1. What is calling you here to this inquiry, right here, right now?

2. What do you believe the world is asking of its leaders now?

3. If you were writing an invitation to yourself, to claim this work, what would it say?

4. Have you taken any standard leadership assessments? What did they reveal to you?

5. Do you have the courage to look at yourself with new and fresh eyes and allow your inquiry to deepen over time?

Wishing you a meaningful journey to self.

_____

_____

_____

_____

_____

_____

_____

"Our work is to make ourselves visible in the world. This is the soul's individual journey, and the soul would much rather fail at its own life than succeed at someone else's."
David Whyte

Reflection #2:
Courage to Be Seen

While the first step of the new leadership path requires self-exploration, the road to your true power also demands the simultaneous willingness and courage to be seen by others. Without this willingness, we will not have the true mirror to see our reflection in the world. Without a true reflection of how we move as leaders and how we show up in the world, we cannot start the process of impacting the world differently. Being seen requires the courage to take off our various masks and let others into our inner sanctum. This courage, in turn, will allow others to experience us fully and will provide an example for them to begin a similar journey. David Whyte (On Being, April 7, 2016) reminds us that people can already see what we're trying to hide. So, the real courage needed is simply to acknowledge the truth that trying to hide is futile. With the courage to be seen, we start a new conversation with the world— and we invite others to be with us fully in that discussion.

1. Does the "being seen" requirement make sense to you?

2. How would you rate your current level of openness? Does any need for perfection stand in your way? How do you resist the temptation to hide?

3. Do you see how being authentically open will add to your ability to be a better leader?

4. Can you think of a person who exhibits this authentic openness? What do they do differently?

5. How will you maintain your undeniable self-worth and confidence while you explore areas for improvement?

Wishing you the courage to be visible today.

"Your soul knows the geography of your destiny. Your soul alone has the map of your future, therefore you can trust this indirect, oblique side of yourself."
John O'Donohue

_____

_____

_____

_____

_____

_____

_____

_____

_____

_____

_____

_____

_____

Your leadership is and will be defined to a great extent by your daily personal language and the way you converse with the world in general. "Hearing" your words and how you use them is one of the first steps to capturing your leadership essence. Harvard Business Review published an article, "Leadership Is a Conversation" (Groysberg & Slind, 2012), wherein they identified the characteristics that go into an impactful leadership conversation. This article, which we review in more depth later in this guidebook, underscored that we should look not only at our words (although they are important) but also the level of intimacy, inclusion, interaction, and intention attached to them. In our transformational journey together, one of our first goals of self-discovery is to bring our full consciousness and intent to the words we use. To raise your language consciousness, we invite you to take a current assessment of the language you use to interact with others on a daily basis.

1. Look at the table on the opposite page and circle all words you frequently use. Are they strong words? Positive? Clear in meaning?

2. Do you choose your words intentionally, or are they remnants of your history and background?

3. What opportunities do you have now to use more intentional and powerful language to drive toward your desired outcomes?

4. How do your words and phrases reflect your leadership values? What do they say about you?

5. Do you find yourself repeating phrases made popular by the latest management trend? (Think outside the box, move the needle).

Wishing you words of your desired intent.

Negative Vocabulary Words				Positive Vocabulary Words			
Angry	Expensive	Negative	Sick	Absolutely	Family	Knowledge	Resilient
Annoyed	Failure	Nonsense	Small	Abundant	Flourishing	Learn	Respectful
Anxious	Faulty	Not	Sorrow	Achieve	Forgive	Love	Results
Apathetic	Fear	Offensive	Spiteful	Action	Free	Mindful	Rewarding
Boring	Fight	Old	Stupid	Admire	Friendly	Motivating	Seek
Broken	Forget	Painful	Sue	Approve	Fun	Moving	Service
Cheap	Frighten	Pessimistic	Suspicious	Beautiful	Funny	New	Smart
Cheat	Gross	Poor	Terrible	Believe	Future	Nuturing	Smile
Control	Guilt	Prejudice	Threatening	Brilliant	Gratitude	Optimistic	Soulful
Corrupt	Hard	Problem	Unfair	Calm	Grow	Peace	Spirit
Criticize	Hate	Rage	Unhappy	Choose	Happy	Please	Spirited
Cruel	Hostile	Reaction	Unhealthy	Courageous	Harmony	Positive	Success
Dark	Hurtful	Reduce	Unjust	Create	Healing	Power	Successful
Difficult	Idiot	Repulsive	Upset	Creative	Heart	Powerful	Supporting
Disease	Jealous	Revenge	Victim	Delightful	Humor	Present	Thanks
Disempower	Lazy	Rude	Vindictive	Dream	Idea	Progress	Transformative
Disgusting	Lose	Rule	War	Easy	Imagine	Promise	Truthful
Dishonest	Loser	Ruthless	Waste	Efficient	Improve	Proud	Unique
Doubt	Malicious	Sad	Weak	Energetic	Include	Quality	Value
Down	Mean	Separate	Worry	Enthusiasm	Innovate	Radiant	Vibrant
Envious	Nasty	Shame	Worse	Excellent	Joy	Release	Welcome

Circle the words which are part of your frequent vocabulary. What impact is your language having on the energy of your team? Write down a word or two that you can commit to being more conscious of how and why you use it.

REFLECTION #4:
YOUR MESSAGE BEYOND WORDS

Although verbal words are important, leadership is also a conversation that begins before, after, and during words. We all convey messages before and after we speak about what we value and what we believe about ourselves. We "speak" as we walk down the hall, sit in meetings, drive our cars, go to the grocery store, and otherwise go throughout our day. Our level of fitness, style of clothing, office interior, place of residence, etc., say many things about us and help form the filter that others hear us through.

Much has been written about communication in leadership. There are many varying statistics about the impact of verbal vs nonverbal messages, but it is clear from all of them that nonverbal cues play an important role in what is communicated. Complicating it further, different cultures interpret nonverbal signals differently. The key, once again, is to be intentional and aware of the receiver, and how our nonverbal messages may be interpreted.

Some of the nonverbal areas we consider are eye contact, hand gestures, tone of voice, appearance, distance, and facial expressions.

1. What are some of the consistent characteristics of your nonverbal messages?

2. Does your message reflect confidence, invitation, or superiority?

3. Are your messages conveying the truth of who you are? How can you get feedback about these messages to guide your awareness?

4. What beliefs, values, and culture may be driving your nonverbal messages?

5. Are there any beliefs that are now invalid, and are no longer serving you?

Wishing you congruity between your heart
and your appearance in the world.

_____

_____

_____

_____

_____

_____

_____

_____

_____

_____

"I know for sure that what we dwell on is who we become."
Oprah Winfrey

REFLECTION #5:
HIGHER PURPOSE

Remarkable leaders are drawn to a higher purpose in their work—something often more permanent and powerful than the actual work product they help produce. These leaders know that people respond to the why of work, and they expose the deeper meaning of the tasks day by day. However, while they do not shy away from the word "purpose," they do recognize that many may find it a daunting concept. Accordingly, they vary their language to include many ways to speak to purpose. They apply purpose principles to common pursuits and help others recognize the value in their work, understanding that employees are no longer satisfied with just coming to work and getting a paycheck...if they ever really were. All of us want to feel something sacred and meaningful in the call to work each day. Leaders help us find that feeling.

1. What pulls you to your own personal effort characterized as your "job?"

2. Do you feel a true connection to a purpose, or are you "settling" for less than your heart's desire?

3. Is your purpose conscious and apparent in your leadership?

4. How do you help others answer the "why am I working here" question?

5. Does your organization publish a compelling "why" through a vision/mission statement or other communication?

Wishing you a closer walk with your purpose today.

"You must learn one thing:
The world was made to be free in. Give up all the other
worlds except the one to which you belong."
David Whyte

_____

_____

_____

_____

_____

_____

_____

_____

_____

_____

_____

_____

_____

_____

REFLECTION #6:
THE POWER OF LISTENING

Conscious leadership calls for a renewed sense of hearing—a listening that goes beyond hearing the words spoken. This type of listening "hears" all that the person is saying through nonverbal messages, history, energy, and what is left unsaid. This enhanced listening is aware of the human filters, biases, and judgements that we all fall prey to when interacting with others. In a world that values speaking above all else, conscious leaders value listening skills in themselves and others, recognizing that they are required to be fully present. These leaders accept that being fully present is the greatest gift they can give to a speaker, and is the first step in improving listening skills. In addition, they understand that power differences affect how we listen and how we are heard. Most important, these leaders create a culture and environment that's ripe for listening by removing hierarchical blocks, asking more questions, creating psychological safety, and preventing the loudest voices to dominate.

1. How do you characterize your level of listening? Do you find yourself distracted and moving ahead of the speaker's words? Can you cite an example of the impact of that distraction?

2. Can you recall a time where you felt truly listened to? What was the impact? How can we help ourselves and others improve in this arena?

3. How can we bring listening into our daily practice of leadership? How can we ask ourselves, "Did I listen well today?" and force ourselves to give examples?

4. How can we build listening into the leadership expectations of our organizations?

Wishing you a day of mindful listening.

"Listening is about being present, not just about being quiet." Krista Tippett

Reflection #7:
Leaders as Teachers

As leaders, we walk into a "classroom" every day, and in some of our most impactful hours we show up as "teachers"—often teaching what we need to learn. However, too often leaders ignore the many ways they teach those they lead—through example, through the priorities they set, the assignments they give, the vision they create, etc. In addition, leaders often teach what they themselves need to learn. It is as if the universe is conspiring to bring the lesson to the student and the teacher simultaneously—keeping the dance of the relationship alive and meaningful. Impactful leaders understand that teaching is not a side activity, but at the very center of their roles. These leaders evolve their teaching skills and methodologies over time to constantly match their diverse audiences. They judge a lot of their success by the growth of their students.

1. How does being a teacher resonate with you?

2. What implicit and explicit lessons are you currently learning and teaching?

3. Do you have the skills to be an effective teacher? What evidence supports your assessment?

4. What are the most important lessons for your organization to learn now? Are the organizational learning priorities clear?

5. What students can you identify that have benefited from your teachings? What did they learn?

May you enjoy every moment as both teacher and student.

"Every one of us gets through the tough times because somebody is there, standing in the gap to close it for us." Oprah Winfrey

REFLECTION #8:
GROWING A CULTURE OF ACCOUNTABILITY

Effective leaders are called upon to build a culture of accountability throughout the organization, beginning with a deep personal ownership of words and actions. These leaders keep track of their commitments and openly admit when they do not meet them. They do not overpromise or overcommit. They understand that continuous failures of accountability destroy their leadership credibility and organizational trust. Throughout the company, they are not afraid to hold others accountable, creating a structure that enables commitment-keeping, as well as providing the trust and clarity that supports accountability. They resist the temptation to only hold accountable when it's safe and comfortable, recognizing that failure to hold accountable is always a disservice to the people they lead. They are clear on their expectations in general, and the organization is consistently reminded through various forms of communications that accountability is a value that is critical to the development of human potential and vital to the organization's success.

1. How do you describe yourself as a leader who drives accountability?

2. What practices do you follow that help you meet your own promises and commitments, both implicit and explicit? How do you respond when you have not met your commitments (something we all experience)?

3. Are you known for overpromising or overcommitting? If so, how can you correct that reputation, starting today?

4. How do you hold others accountable for meeting their commitments? How do you respond when they don't? Describe a situation where you held someone accountable successfully?

5. How successful have you been at building a culture of accountability? What worked and what didn't?

Wishing you the courage to hold yourself and others accountable.

_____

_____

_____

_____

_____

_____

_____

_____

_____

_____

_____

_____

_____

_____

_____

_____

_____

_____

_____

_____

_____

_____

REFLECTION #9:
MASCULINE AND FEMININE BALANCE

Leaders who build powerful cultures recognize the need to balance the feminine with the masculine energies throughout the organization. While they work to balance their own personal energy, they also recognize that employees may authentically express one of these two archetypal energies more than the other. These leaders know that the language of "feminine and masculine energy" may seem foreign to some and they use models like the one on the opposite page to explain it in practical terms. They encourage conversation about the value of both and they address how gender stereotypes may have thwarted the goal of balance in the organization. They expose when discrimination emerges, and they reinforce the notion that a balance of positive feminine and masculine leadership traits results in greater organizational success. In addition, they expose the downsides to both hyper-femininity and hyper-masculinity. These leaders are certain that only balance can lead to the right work getting done in the right way.

1. Can you identify different masculine and feminine ways of working?

2. Do you consciously seek a balance of both on teams and on projects?

3. Are you building appreciation for both perspectives and making sure that both voices are being heard?

4. How do you use masculine energy in your leadership today? How do you use feminine energy in your leadership today?

5. How do you build an awareness of and remedy for hyper-masculinity and hyper-femininity?

Wishing you a day of energetic balance.

Masculine and Feminine Power Traits

RELEASING POWER

FEMININE	MASCULINE

Empathy, Inclusion, Intuition, Collaboration, Vulnerability, Harmony, Patience, Creativity	Action, Clarity, Assertiveness, Focus, Confidence, Discipline, Execution, Decisiveness
Dependence, Neediness, Distraction, Irrationality, Weakness, Manipulation, Submissiveness, Smothering	Aggression, Ego, Cruelty, Control, Arrogance, Insensitivity, Intolerance, Domination

BLOCKING POWER

"If any human being is to reach full maturity both the masculine and feminine sides of the personality must be brought up into consciousness." M. Esther Harding

REFLECTION #10:
CONTAGIOUS COURAGE

Remarkable leaders often demonstrate a great deal of courage—the ability to move beyond their fears and demonstrate behavior that in turn helps free others from their fears and encourages boldness in the organization. This courage shows up in their personal leadership attributes and in the organizational strategy. The fearlessness of these leaders is contagious—so much so that the people around them move in response to the leaders' way of being, often without even knowing why. Remarkable leaders create an environment that accepts failure as a part of learning while encouraging appropriate risktaking throughout the organization. They value courageous people, but the organization knows the leaders also require the ability to be humbly brave. They have real conversations about how fear gets in the way of innovation and creativity and authenticity. While they define courage in many actions, these leaders know that showing up authentically and vulnerability every day is often the bravest act of all.

1. What is the most courageous thing you have ever done?
   (Personal or business)

2. What personal fears can you still identify? Are these personal fears holding you back from your highest good and grandest impact?

3. What progress have you made in moving past these fears?

4. How do you build courage throughout the organization? How do you address organizational failure and truth telling?

5. How do you model and encourage vulnerability and authenticity as a sign of courage?

Wishing you a day of demonstrating courage.

"Courage doesn't always roar. Sometimes courage is the quiet voice at the end of the day saying, 'I will try again tomorrow.'" Mary Anne Radmache

REFLECTION #11:
PHYSICAL WELLNESS

A conscious leader understands the impact physical wellness has on the ability to lead. These leaders emanate energy and wholeness and know that having a strong, flexible, and energetic physical body facilitates a strong, flexible, and energetic leadership mind. Conversely, an abused and neglected body often leads to weak, confused, or undisciplined leadership. This physical health focus includes a commitment to healthy nutrition, physical activity, and stress management. Leaders who do not take care of their personal wellness often do not demonstrate a commitment to organizational wellness. This lack of commitment will have a negative impact on the ability of the organization to manage stress and change. Leaders who lead effectively know that strong physical bodies form the foundation of all other aspects of wellness, and they build wellness into the company culture. Quite simply, people who are strong and healthy create a more "alive" and vibrant workplace and organization.

1. What are your thoughts about physical wellness and the connection to strong leadership?

2. How do you model physical wellness for those you lead?

3. What changes can you make right here, right now, to enhance your physical health?

4. What habits could you eliminate right now to increase your physical well-being? What is stopping you?

5. What programs have you implemented to support organizational wellness? What others could you implement to bolster physical wellness?

Wishing you a long and healthy life experience.

"Health is a state of body. Wellness is a state of being." J. Stanford

REFLECTION #12:
CREATING AND MAINTAINING A COMPELLING VISION/MISSION

Transformational leaders understand the importance of a real and compelling vision/mission that originates from or is reaffirmed by the people within the organization. Based on this understanding, these leaders take the time to create a workflow for the development of the organizational purpose that can stand the test of time. They do not consider this as a "nice to do" activity or a "have to do" burden, but they see it as central to their leadership. These leaders recognize that the words printed on the wall to capture the organizational purpose must go beyond intellect and touch the emotional center of employees. In addition, the vision/mission must be inclusive enough to allow every employee to see himself or herself in it. Transformational leaders understand that a vision/mission can be empty words on a poster or can truly drive culture and performance. These leaders use the vision in everyday language and translate how it should show up in everyday action. This vision and mission then become central to the organizational spirit.

1. Is your vision/mission compelling and still valid today? Does it inspire you?

2. Can your team recite its vision/mission without reading it? Did they help develop it or reaffirm it?

3. What are the visible signs of the vision/mission in the organization?

4. How does your leadership regularly confirm the organizational purpose?

5. What opportunities exist today for you to impact the ongoing vision/mission of your organization?

May you bring your vision and mission to life today.

REFLECTION #13:
NAVIGATING AN INTERGENERATIONAL WORKFORCE

Today's leaders are faced with a workforce that is comprised of different generations and varying value systems. With the trends of retiring later and less adherence to hierarchy, the traditional models of power are being displaced. No longer is the most experienced person the most knowledgeable or the most valued. As a result, organizations are forced to set up new rules of engagement and new norms related to authority. In addition, as the various generations work more closely together, the impact of unconscious bias can be more significant with different generations. Younger workers may dismiss older workers as stuck in their ways and closed-minded, while older workers will view younger colleagues as entitled, tech-obsessed, and overly-challenging of norms or rules. In order to effectively manage an intergenerational workforce, leaders must recognize the gifts of all age groups and work to address value differences while meeting overall organizational objectives.

1. What generations are represented in your workforce? Is there a dominant generation?

2. What structure is in place to retain and engage employees of all ages?

3. What challenges does your organization face with the new blended workforce?

4. How are you dealing with value differences and differing work and learning practices?

5. How do you show respect and reward contributions from your intergenerational workforce?

Wishing you a harmonious workforce of all ages.

"The people who shape our lives and our cultures have the ability to communicate a vision or a quest or a joy or a mission." Tony Robbins

Reflection #14:
Innovation Catalyst

Transformational leaders pursue a forward-thinking mindset in themselves and others. They accept that people and organizations are designed to create, evolve, and renew, and they build cultures that are curious and exploring. This curiosity leads to continual innovation and a removal of "sacred cows" that keep an organization stagnant. These leaders reward employees for questioning the status quo, and they find ways to build innovation into daily operations. They don't settle for the "if it's not broke, don't fix it" mentality. They promote and reward "breakthrough thinking" and innovation at all levels, not just in the technical domain. They also create a psychological space where employees feel safe to explore and offer new ideas. These leaders live with and learn from failures and recognize them as a part of an innovating culture. Finally, they invest time, money, and other resources in the pursuit of innovation, and they search for ways to expose themselves and others to innovative thinkers. They don't limit their connections to people in their industries, they seek inspiration from anywhere it exists.

1. In what areas of your organization do you settle for the "status quo?"

2. How do you create an environment where employees feel safe to challenge old ways of thinking?

3. In what ways do you model innovation in your own life and work?

4. How are you investing time, money, and resources into the pursuit of innovation?

5. What incentives or rewards do you have in place in your organization to support innovation?

Wishing you a life filled with curiosity and creation.

"Without leaps of imagination, or dreaming, we lose the excitement of possibilities. Dreaming, after all, is a form of planning." Gloria Steinem

REFLECTION #15:
LEADERSHIP AS A PROFESSION

Impactful leaders embrace the truth that leadership is both an art and a science—a skilled profession to be studied, practiced, and mastered—with a goal toward an effectiveness that is measurable. These leaders follow great leaders, read books and other publications, and take developmental classes and workshops. They constantly seek feedback from a variety of sources, especially from those they lead. These leaders don't "wing it," they know that leadership is a sacred and honorable profession, and they know the people they lead deserve their best. Impactful leaders know they can no longer rely solely on their subject matter expertise while neglecting their leadership mandate. The seek balance between expanding operational and leadership knowledge. They are willing to focus on and create environments that assign value to leadership activities such as coaching, mentoring, and self-reflection. They do not assign value solely to production.

1. What can you identify in your leadership journey that demonstrates your study of leadership?

2. How informed and excited are you about the latest research and findings on leadership? Who are some of your favorite "experts" on the subject?

3. What measurements do you use to gauge your leadership progress?

4. What work could you commit to–right here, right now–to more wholly own the title of "leader?"

5. How are you modeling leadership development for the organization?

May you always acknowledge the power of a leadership profession.

_____

_____

_____

REFLECTION #16
DISPLAYING VULNERABILITY

The courage to be vulnerable as a leader has received a great deal of attention in recent years. Notably, Brene Brown began public discourse on this topic in 2010 with a now-famous Ted Talk that centered around shame and vulnerability. Her research and others like it underscored that the ability to be vulnerable is the foundation of all trusting relationships, and by extension, trusting leadership. Inspirational leaders have an ability to be vulnerable in a way that motivates those around them to also show up as their most authentic selves, and transforms the idea of vulnerability from a weakness to a strength. These leaders display vulnerability by asking questions and freely admitting when they need help or have made mistakes. They have faith in the ability of their teams to accept them as their leader without the need to be perfect, all-knowing, or invincible. These leaders know that covering up restricts them, as well as the organization, from internal growth. They own their personal stories and they give others freedom to do the same.

1. What is your first reaction to the word "vulnerability?" What have you been taught about it?

2. How do you now see value in demonstrating vulnerability?

3. How would your team describe your ability to be vulnerable?

4. What effort are you making to create a safe environment for others to display vulnerability?

5. Detail your most courageous moment of vulnerability. What prompted you? How did you move through it?

Wishing you the courage to own and tell your own perfect, imperfect story.

"Vulnerability sounds like truth and feels like courage. Truth and courage aren't always comfortable, but they're never weakness."

Brene Brown

Effective leaders are skilled at managing both the "healthy" and the "smart" aspects of their organizations. They are focused on getting things done in a manner that uplifts the organization in a sustainable way. While they understand that they must deliver financial results to be a strong leader, they pay equal attention to maintaining a thriving culture and overall organizational wellness. They balance the "being" and the "doing" of the organization in practice. These leaders believe that you don't need to sacrifice healthy for smart, or vice versa, and they accept the evidence that healthy organizations actually deliver superior results. Finally, they also know that lack of clarity destroys the health of the organization and they work daily to eliminate confusion within the organization. These leaders do not delegate organizational health but see it as central to their leadership responsibilities. Patrick Lencioni captured this idea in his *Advantage* model (2012) with the traits listed below . The ultimate organizational goal is always balanced.

Smart	Healthy
Products & Services	High Clarity
Strategy	Low Politics
Market	Low Turnover
Technology	High Morale
Finances	Flexibility
Technical Skills	Customer Satisfaction

1. How do you divide your time between "healthy" and "smart?"

2. Is your organization more skilled in one category, or is it quite balanced?

3. How does your strategic plan support both sides of the healthy/ smart equation?

4. What key performance indicators (KPIs) does the organization follow that demonstrate the organizational commitment to healthy/smart?

5. How are leaders assessed in their capacity to lead both areas?

Wishing you a healthy and smart organization.

_____

_____

_____

_____

_____

_____

_____

_____

_____

_____

_____

_____

_____

_____

_____

_____

_____

_____

_____

_____

_____

REFLECTION # 18:
CHANGE LEADERSHIP

Successful leaders accept that "leading change" is a central and essential part of their assignment as a leader. To be effective at leading change, they utilize the skills of assessing the current state accurately and completely while simultaneously and inspirationally defining the desired "future state." These leaders never try to soften the issues that exist today—they insist on reality. But at the same time, they optimistically declare the possibilities for tomorrow. They also recognize that emotional resistance to change is to be expected, and they help others navigate through the various stages of change (denial, resistance, anger, acceptance). They reframe change as part of a dynamic corporate culture, and they incorporate it as a routine fixture of work while underscoring the need to accomplish change with mastery. These leaders study and speak openly about change and they walk through change hand in hand with the organization.

1. What methodology do you use to make an assessment about the current state of a project, department, or company, to know what needs to change and why?

2. How inspirational are you at declaring a "future state?" How do you make the future state look worthy of enduring the discomfort of change?

3. How do you deal with the emotional aspects of change for yourself and for others?

4. What has been your proudest "change leadership" moment?

5. What support might you need to become more expert at steering between "current" and "future" states and leading change between the two?

Wishing you exciting and effective change experiences.

_____

_____

_____

_____

_____

_____

_____

_____

_____

_____

_____

_____

_____

_____

"We all want things to stay the same. Settle for living in misery because we are afraid of change, of things crumbling to ruins. Ruin is a gift. Ruin is the road to transformation." Elizabeth Gilbert

REFLECTION #19:
KNOW YOUR BUSINESS

Prosperous leaders understand that effectively describing an inspirational and meaningful "future state" requires a deep understanding of world, industry, and company trends. To accomplish this, they incorporate into their daily work conversations the study of their businesses and evolving impacts to it. These leaders see trends before they are reported on, and they synthesize this data for their employees with a sense of excitement. They determine what impacts these trends might have on their teams, and communicate frequently on potential issues. Their teams learn from them, while at the same time being held accountable for their individual growth and level of market expertise. These leaders invest in activities that support greater market knowledge and they support employees' efforts to increase their knowledge, as well. With this collective expertise, everyone develops a deeper sense of ownership for organizational success.

1. How do you keep abreast of your industry and the trends affecting it?

2. How do you make complex business realties accessible to varying levels of understanding?

3. Would others describe you as having expertise in your industry? What specific expertise would they attribute to you?

4. What evidence can you point to that your teams have a practice of industry exploration? How do you measure it?

5. How do you bring curiosity and wonder about your business into the daily workflow?

Wishing you the business acumen to conquer new frontiers.

Effective leaders understand that today's teams are overloaded with mass information and competing objectives, and they fully appreciate that noise is literally coming at employees from all directions. These leaders know that their ability to set clear and consistent priorities is as important as declaring and repeatedly articulating the vision that underpins those priorities. They are committed to helping the organization synthesize information and discern what is important now. They bring clarity every day to what their teams must pay attention to, and they create alignment around their key objectives to avoid conflict among team members. Effective leaders also help the organization become more skilled at data use and management to prevent information overload. They know that less is often more, and they know that distilling information to make it actionable is a key charge of their leadership.

1. How do you determine the quantity and type of information you pay attention to every day? Do you struggle to "hit delete" to minimize information clutter?

2. How do you set the stage for clear priorities and help direct the organization to the data that is most important for the organization's strategic plan?

3. What tools do you use to maintain focus and eliminate data distraction?

4. How you do remain faithful to your priorities when "emergencies" and other opportunities arise?

5. How do you determine and measure whether alignment on priorities is maintained throughout the organization amid growing data and distractions?

Wishing you a day of focus and clarity.

"With clarity of direction, the inability to make decisions can disappear."
John Kotter

Breakthrough leaders know how to manage conflict—a typical component of a fast-moving, forward-thinking company which is implementing many projects, with a strong diversity of people. These leaders know that healthy conflict is a normal part of the creative process but also understand that unhealthy conflict can undermine the trust level of the organization. On a personal level, they are conscious of their own natural response to and style of conflict, and they work hard to reinterpret conflict to build alignment in the organization and achieve superior ideas. To maintain this creative tension, breakthrough leaders focus on establishing a culture that views vigorous debate as a part of the alignment process. They explain to the organization that conflict is needed to get to the best result, and they demonstrate comfort with debate and challenge. They explain to the organization the difference between alignment and agreement. These leaders watch for boring meetings and lack of alignment to assess whether their teams have mastered healthy conflict. On other hand, they do not permit organizational debate to become personal, and they deal with interpersonal issues directly and swiftly.

1. How do you rate your comfort level with conflict in general? What is your natural approach to conflict: collaborator, avoider, compromiser, or combater?

2. How have you built a framework for healthy conflict in the past? What was the result?

3. How do you effectively build trust to support conflict?

4. How do you manage the various conflict approaches of your team members–making sure that despite styles, each voice is heard?

5. How do you make the nature of the conflict and the resolution of

it transparent? How do you insist on alignment when agreement doesn't occur?

Wishing you a day of healthy debates.

_____

_____

_____

_____

_____

_____

_____

"When there is trust, conflict becomes nothing but the pursuit
of truth, an attempt to find the best possible answer."
Patrick Lencioni

REFLECTION #22: BUILDING TRUST

Transformational leaders know that the ability of a company to transform in any area is dependent on the level of trust that exists in their organization. They measure trust and embed trust-building components into their daily consciousness and work plan. They don't view the ability to generate trust as a "soft skill" or a "nice to do." Rather, they see it as being central to their leadership. Organizationally, the pursuit of building trust is evident in their communications and their meetings. To bring clarity to the concept of "trust," leaders provide simple models and definitions for the "how to" of trust building. They include the responsibility of being trustworthy and trusting others. We use a representative model below to depict three characteristics that form the foundation of a trusting environment but recognize that the conversation of trust can depend on the culture and the organization. We hold that building trust is a learnable skill and should be part of leadership development and assessed competencies.

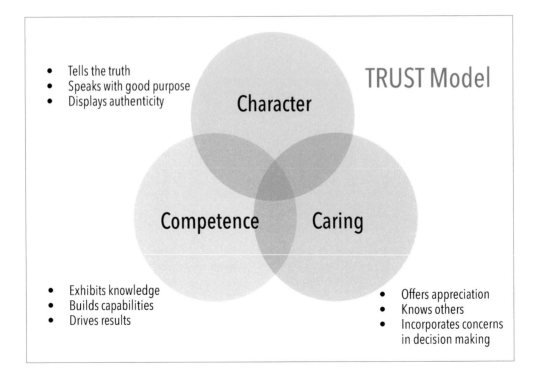

TRUST Model

- Tells the truth
- Speaks with good purpose
- Displays authenticity

Character

Competence

- Exhibits knowledge
- Builds capabilities
- Drives results

Caring

- Offers appreciation
- Knows others
- Incorporates concerns in decision making

1. Review the model and identify your personal strengths and weaknesses.

2. Do you have any current actions or practices that could be barriers to character, competency, or caring?

3. What is the current conversation around trust-building in your organization? How do you measure the level of trust? Are there areas of broken trust?

4. What core beliefs were you taught about trusting others? How were you educated about trust in general?

5. How can you now help your organization understand the role of trust in getting work done and meeting organizational objectives?

Wishing you a day of healthy debates.

_____

_____

_____

_____

_____

_____

_____

_____

_____

_____

_____

REFLECTION #23:
CREATING CONNECTIONS

Inspirational leaders know that the ability to connect—truly connect—with others is an essential part of the trust-building and leadership process. They have the ability to "know" themselves and others in a way that creates community and unity. At the same time, they understand there isn't just one formula for connection, and they allow space for themselves and others to discover their own paths to connection. They also acknowledge that connecting is a skill to be practiced and learned, and a foundational aspect of doing power differently. Inspirational leaders accept that there is no "faking it" in the pursuit of human connection, and they learn to be comfortable with the discomfort true connection can evoke. They are willing to risk rejection and status, and they initiate connecting conversations with intent. These leaders review their ability to connect as part of their own leadership development, and they purposely expand their circles year after year, seeking out people who bring different perspectives and have various backgrounds and experiences.

1. How are you pursuing connection with others?

2. How have you experienced personal connections–or lack thereof– impacting your daily work life?

3. What is the current organizational expectation around authentically connecting with others?

4. How do you deal with an inability to connect with someone who is important to your mission?

5. How have you grown over the years in your capacity to be with others and connect with them?

Wishing you strong and powerful connections.

"Successful people become great leaders w hen they learn to shift the focus from themselves to others." Marshall Goldsmith

_____

_____

_____

_____

_____

_____

_____

_____

_____

_____

_____

_____

_____

REFLECTION #24:
DRIVING OPERATIONAL IMPROVEMENTS

Remarkable leaders are often propelled by a drive to improve something, to leave a situation better than they found it, and to inscribe their indelible mark on a place or time. This impulse drives operational improvements and other organizational enhancements. The desire, however, is not ego-based. Rather, it comes from a reservoir that insists on contributing to the world. Leaders who achieve operational improvements through others inspire the same passion within those employees to make things more efficient or effective. They also understand that driving continuous operational improvements requires both vision and workflow mastery. In other words, the "why" and the "how" of these improvements are front and center as they are being pursued. The drive for improvement also requires a strong commitment to employee empowerment—the people who do the work often know the best way to improve it. Finally, it recognizes the option that outside experts may also have a role to play in exposing where opportunities for operational improvements lie. Leaders who strive for this extraordinary excellence bring the mindset that there is always room for improvement.

1. What successes can you identify where you have significantly contributed to "fixing things" in the past?

2. What key improvements or programs are you pursuing now? Is anything getting in the way?

3. What need or vision is driving your efforts? How do you communicate them?

4. What has been the impact of your operational improvements? When they are negative, how do you communicate the continuing need to pursue them? How do you identify and communicate the root causes of issues so that you are not fixing the same thing over and over?

5. How do you build ownership throughout the organization for operational improvement?

May you have the vision and mastery for continuous improvement.

_____

_____

_____

_____

_____

_____

_____

_____

_____

_____

_____

_____

"Never interrupt someone doing what you said couldn't be done." Amelia Earhart

REFLECTION #25:
YOUR LEADERSHIP STORY

Your leadership perspective is based subconsciously on how you were introduced to and what you were taught about leadership. Your religion, your early heroes, your family structure, your role models, your early school experience, your first job, what you watched and what you read all play a role. Knowing these influencers and uncovering their messages can help accelerate your leadership development by letting you determine what you hold to be true and what serves you now. For instance, what were you taught about the role and responsibilities of authority? Were you allowed to question authority? In your experience, what was the origin of power for leaders? What was the balance of speaking and listening of that leadership? Knowing and owning our own leadership stories and the core beliefs that made them provides a pathway to a new way of thinking and experiencing leadership.

1. What was your first encounter with power and leadership? What interactions stood out?

2. Who in your life played a significant role in forming your ideas of leadership?

3. What teachers stand out for you? What do you remember about them?

4. What was your first leadership role? What drew you to it? How has your approach changed over time?

5. What significant emotional events have you had as a leader or with a leader? What aspects of your leadership are you most proud of?

Wishing you an evolving leadership story.

"Let the beauty we love be what we do. There are hundreds
of ways to kneel and kiss the ground."
Rumi

REFLECTION #26:
DEVELOPING GRIT & RESILIENCE

Leaders who achieve extraordinary results often have well-developed muscles of grit and resilience—the ability to stay with a goal, move through the hurdles of life, and get back up quickly when they fall. Angela Lee Duckworth studied grit in a variety of circumstances, including the classroom, corporations, sports, and parenting, and found that grit played a critical role in ultimate success. She defined grit as the passion and perseverance for long-term goals and determined that it was a more important determinant of success than IQ. Similarly, resilient leaders move with confidence because they know they can overcome daunting challenges. They have a demonstrated belief that they are stronger than their circumstances. Exceptional leaders teach and model this resilience in their daily lives, and they are proud to tell their "rising above it" stories. Because they know they can get back up, they explore many things others would avoid. They also do not wallow in "woe is me." They believe Ralph Waldo Emerson's quote, "Our greatest glory is not in never failing, but in rising up every time we fail." Accordingly, they do not live in fear nor flinch when challenge arises. They trust fully in their ability to be resilient and the organization's capacity for overcoming challenges.

1. Do you describe yourself as resilient? What evidence do you have that supports that characterization?

2. Are you authentically proud of the hurdles you have faced in life? Have you told those stories?

3. How would you describe your level of "grit?" What long-term goal have you pursued over time?

4. Who do you know that is an example of grit and resilience? How do they use those traits in their leadership?

5. What challenges has your organization overcome? How do you use that experience in your organization narrative?

Here's to every experience that has made you stronger.

_____

_____

_____

_____

_____

_____

_____

_____

_____

_____

"I can be changed by what happens to me. But I refuse to be reduced by it."
Maya Angelou

Strong leaders often have an abundance of energy, which stems from a practice of engaging with activities that lift them up and avoiding people and experiences that drain them. They know what supports and what depletes their enthusiasm and optimism, and they are conscious of what circumstances affect energy levels. Because they know what impacts them, they intentionally manage those things. While they recognize they can't eliminate negativity, mindful leaders protect their energy as a priceless leadership asset. That doesn't mean they don't expose themselves or take emotional risks—they do. They are just mindful when people, job, circumstances, or situations no longer serve them, and they resist the temptation to ignore the situation. These leaders also understand that home and work are interrelated, and what happens in one domain impacts the other. They have a purposeful and holistic approach to managing their physical, emotional, mental, and spiritual energy in their everyday lives. They, in turn, distribute this energy throughout the organization.

1. How would you describe your energy level today? This week? In general?

2. How do you notice when your energy is going up or down?

3. Do you purposefully take note of energy drains (those things and people that "suck the life out of you")? Do you intentionally eliminate them or move through them quickly?

4. What practice do you have to help you increase or maintain your energy levels?

5. How would others describe your energy impact on the organization?

Wishing you a day filled with vim and vigor!

_____

_____

_____

_____

_____

_____

_____

_____

_____

_____

_____

_____

_____

_____

_____

_____

_____

_____

_____

_____

_____

_____

_____

_____

REFLECTION #28:
PERSONAL INTEGRITY

Trusted leaders understand the role that personal integrity plays in the credibility and effectiveness of their leadership. They accept that "who you are" is as important as "what you do" when you lead people. These leaders know integrity requires alignment between what they say and what they do and encompasses truthfulness, respect, and doing the right thing even when no one is watching. They are clear what the word "integrity" means to them, and when they fall short of their personal integrity expectations, they quickly own their actions and adjust their behaviors. Trusted leaders insist on a culture of integrity in their organizations, and they exhibit zero tolerance for violations of integrity. They do not exaggerate their own successes, but praise others' contributions and hold themselves accountable to the entire organization. Leaders with integrity strengthen the business and minimize risk to the investment. Companies with ethical management enhance their abilities to attract investors, engage more successfully with customers, and attract better talent. These leaders interpret integrity to include living with general moral principles.

1. How would you describe what the word "integrity" means to you?

2. When have you fallen short of your own expectations? What action did you take?

3. What life lessons have shaped your beliefs about integrity?

4. How does your integrity show up in your daily leadership?

5. What processes and practices are in place to monitor integrity in your operations?

With respect for integrity objectives.

"Integrity is choosing courage over comfort; choosing what is right over what is fun, fast or easy; and choosing to practice our values rather than simply professing them."

Brene Brown

REFLECTION #29:
MOOD AND MORALE

Transformational leaders stay in tune with and intentionally manage their own moods and the morale of the organization. Mood is often defined as the individual state of mind or feelings, while morale is thought of as the confidence, enthusiasm, and discipline of a group at a particular time. The mood of an individual can influence the morale of an organization in subtle and overt ways. We investigate the mood/morale lens with an inquiry: Is it productive or non-productive? What assessments are present that are driving it? Leaders realize that improving mood and morale isn't something you "fix" once and you are finished. Rather, it requires attention to the system of beliefs and attitudes in the organization that must be stoked and uplifted over time. These leaders listen and watch for signs of "M&M" as a part of their daily organizational assessment and they create structures in the organization to help manage them. These structures can take the form of culture clubs, employee resource groups, event groups, etc., but leaders don't depend on these resources to own culture initiatives. They hold themselves and other leaders accountable for the corporate culture and morale. Mindful leaders find a way to measure these important factors of organizational success before an issue arises.

1. How would you describe your mood in this particular place and time using the table provided? What is driving your mood?

2. How would you describe the morale of the organization? What is underlying it?

3. Have you ever had the experience of effectively managing mood and morale? What actions did you take?

4. Are there key people in your organization who influence mood and morale more than others? What is your interaction with those people?

5. Are there actions you could take today to elevate the morale of the organization? Whose help would you need? What first step could you take?

Wishing you the skill to discern and influence mood and morale.

_____

_____

_____

_____

_____

_____

_____

Mood Descriptions

Aggravated	Cheerful	Discontent	Grumpy	Mad	Relaxed
Alone	Calm	Drained	Happy	Melancholy	Relieved
Amused	Cold	Ecstatic	High	Moody	Rejuvenated
Angry	Complacent	Eager	Hopeful	Numb	Restless
Annoyed	Confused	Energetic	Hyper	Optimistic	Respectful
Anxious	Content	Engaged	Impressed	Open	Sad
Apathetic	Cranky	Envious	Indifferent	Peaceful	Satisfied
Ashamed	Curious	Excited	Infuriated	Pessimistic	Stressed
Bitchy	Cynical	Exhausted	Intimidated	Poised	Sympathetic
Bitter	Appreciative	Frustrated	Jealous	Powerful	Thankful
Blah	Depressed	Fulfilled	Lazy	Productive	Tired
Blissful	Determined	Gloomy	Lethargic	Reflective	Uncomfortable
Bored	Disappointed	Grateful	Lonely	Rejected	

Circle the five words which most describe your daily mood at work.
What impact is your mood having on the morale of your team?

REFLECTION #30:
LOVE IN THE WORKPLACE

Effective leaders are completely comfortable with the word "love" and understand the role it plays in corporate success. They interpret this word "love" to mean a deep caring and concern for the lives they lead and influence. They intuitively know that love drives performance—whether it is the love of family, love of community, or the love of country, love underlies the work effort. Love includes showing empathy, listening carefully, expressing appreciation, and displaying a concern for the whole person. That doesn't mean these leaders don't take hard action and make difficult decisions; these leaders understand that love sometimes means saying "no." Conscious leaders drive a culture of love, and they are able to explain its meaning and demonstrate its power in the corporate context. They fully recognize that employees spend much of their time at work, and if love isn't present in the workplace it is absent from a majority of our lives. These leaders have experienced how love can build teamwork, improve performance, and bring greater meaning to the business battlefield. Because they accept that organizations can be the most toxic places on earth or the most rewarding, they embrace love for what it includes: compassion, respect, appreciation, forgiveness, etc., and accept that the power of love is there whether it is acknowledged or not.

1. How is love demonstrated in your leadership? How comfortable are you with expressing it?

2. Can you embrace the idea that love says "no" as often as it says "yes?" What actions have you taken that were difficult but still within the framework of love?

3. What organizational behaviors support a culture of love? How do you build them into an accountability framework?

4. What words or phrases can substitute for the word "love?" Are you comfortable using them?

5. How have you seen the power of love utilized in the workplace?

Wishing you the power of love.

"Great leaders may be found at the top of the mountain looking back
upon their challenges, but the greatest leaders are often found at the
foot of that mountain still helping others reach that summit."
Robert Clancy

Trusted leaders understand that all work is done through relationships, and they cultivate the relationships they need to achieve breakthrough results. They assess the status of their important relationships, and they view relationship-building as part of their leadership responsibilities. These leaders embed this relationship work as part of their individual and company business plans, and they articulate the role relationships play in meeting those plans. These leaders identify the skills that go into relationship-building (authenticity, appreciation, trust, listening, connecting, etc.), and they connect the dots for others to understand the role of each. They do acknowledge that different levels of relationships are required depending on the objectives being pursued, and they embed "business purpose" into a larger discussion of workplace health. This relationship-building is not manipulative but gives honor to the power of relationships in achieving results. Quite simply, work done between people with strong relationships is more efficient and more effective.

1. How conscious are you of the relationships you need to achieve your desired business results? Can you distinguish between manipulative and honorable relationship-building?

2. Do you assess your progress in these relationships as a part of your periodic assessments?

3. What skills do you use to establish and maintain authentic and powerful relationships? Are there skills you need to enhance?

4. How do you use these skills and relationships to get work done?

5. How can you bring more connection to the role of relationships with the ability to work more efficiently and effectively?

Wishing you powerful connections.

Inspirational leaders have an infectious curiosity for life, and they seek to find the deeper layers within people, events, and movements. These leaders can be found reading about new topics, trying new adventures, and meeting new people—all driven by a desire to uncover or discover. In her book, *Big Magic: Creative Living Beyond Fear*, Elizabeth Gilbert states, "Passion is a tower of flame, but curiosity is a tiny tap on the shoulder—a little whisper in the ear that says, 'Hey, that's kind of interesting.' ... Passion is rare; curiosity is every day" (Gilbert, 2015). She goes on to explain that curiosity can be a friend that teaches us how to become more of who we truly are. Inspirational leaders are not afraid to step outside their comfort zone to explore that which they have never experienced. They know curiosity drives breakthrough results and innovation. As Bernard Baruch said, "Millions saw the apple fall, but Newton asked why."

1. Would you describe yourself as curious? What are you curious about now?

2. How does curiosity impact your life? How do you inject it into your organization?

3. What are some things you have discovered in the last week? The last month? The last year?

4. Are you inspired or motivated by figuring things out? How often do you use the words "Can you imagine?" "What if?"

5. Are there ways to add more "seeking and searching" to your life and leadership?

Wishing you a curious mind and heart.

"If we could see the world through the eyes of a child, we would see the magic in everything." Chee Vai Tang

_____

_____

_____

_____

_____

_____

_____

_____

_____

_____

_____

_____

REFLECTION #33:
WARRIOR ENERGY

Effective leaders know that their "warrior energy" must be called upon from time to time to achieve a desired outcome. Whether for our companies, for our communities, or for our country, sometimes the warrior energy is the only energy powerful enough to right a wrong, override injustice, or eradicate inequality. This internal force will compel our genius and wisdom to emerge. It will not accept mediocrity or excuses. Warrior energy can be ignited through a school shooting, the revelation of an abuse of power by a doctor, being forced to ride in the back of the bus, experiencing unequal treatment by law enforcement, or a public demeaning in a corporate setting—literally anything that triggers a strong emotional response or crushes your spirit. Your inner warrior is disciplined and focused, and it will not be deterred by challenge or controversy. It fights for what it believes in, and it refuses to back down. At the same time, effective warriors are not bitter or consumed by this energy. As author Juan Carlos Marcos underscores in his book *Warriors at the Helm: The Leader's Guide to Success in Business*, "Warrior leaders exude positive energy rather than being consumed by negatives. They recognize the problem, deal with it, look for the lessons learned, and move on in a positive manner." Warriors go to war slowly, but they don't deny that option.

1. Do you know your warrior energy? How do you use it?

2. Does your warrior live peacefully with your other leadership attributes? Does it ever try to dominate?

3. Can you point to times in your leadership when no other spirit would propel the organization?

4. Have you ever overused your warrior energy? Can you keep it in balance?

5. How would you characterize your own special brand of warrior?

What other word can you use for that bold leadership if this word doesn't resonate with you?

With deep respect for all the faces of leadership you bring to your organization and to the world.

_____

_____

_____

_____

_____

_____

_____

_____

_____

_____

"Warriors confront the evil that most people refuse to acknowledge."
Bohdi Sanders

REFLECTION #34:
THE SERVICE OF LEADERSHIP

Transformational leaders understand that service is the center of higher leadership. These leaders elevate the status of service throughout the organization, and they demonstrate that no task is beneath them. This passion for service can be seen visibly in organizational operations and through their philanthropy and other acts of kindness, all of which are delivered with humility. They seek balance in the times they are being served with the time they spend serving, ignoring hierarchical norms. They embrace a servant leadership model because they truly believe that service is the highest honor. They consistently ask, "Have I served well today?" From their leadership, service emerges as an authentic value throughout the organization, and it is felt in their culture and in the company's brand.

1. How do you define the word "service?"

2. What were you taught growing up about people who serve?

3. How does the value of service show up in your own life? Would people describe you as a servant-leader?

4. Does the group or organization you lead discuss the goal of service and how they can improve it?

5. What opportunity do you have to help build a greater passion for service in your organization?

May you experience the joy of service.

Reflection #35: Fostering Imagination

Organizations often ignore one of the most valuable human attributes available to it—the power of imagination. As Albert Einstein emphasized, "Imagination is more important than knowledge because knowledge is ultimately limited. Imagination embraces the whole world." Imagination allows the creation of what does not exist, and it propels us to do what is thought of as impossible.

Clearly, organizations that have had the most impact over time have been the most creative and imaginative. From Apple to Tesla to Amazon to Netflix, we know who they are. They don't depend on copying other organizations' products or services—they walk into and chart unknown territory. They can withstand public criticism and skepticism. People like Steve Jobs (or insert your favorite innovator) have proven that the imagination of one individual can spark a significant change the world. Transformational leaders accept that increasing imagination enlarges possibilities, and that an organization without imagination is destined for stagnation. Accordingly, these leaders work to develop their own imaginations, understanding that part of their job is to see a future that is not yet here. Also, imaginative leaders know the clearer you can see, touch, and feel this potential future, the more compellingly you can communicate it to others.

In *The Origin of Leaders*, "Imagination—Developing Your Most Powerful Human Talent" (Neill, 2010), Conor Neill offered ways to develop your imagination:

- Spend time bored
- Read fiction. Write a new ending to a classic book. Make a hero into a villain, and a villain into a hero. Write yourself into the book
- Throw photos on the floor and then explain the connection between them
- Watch TV in another language and explain to a friend what is happening

- Visualize a horse with a sheep's coat and a dolphin's head. Imagine a rubber car
- List ten small improvements you could make to the seat you are sitting on
- Tell bedtime stories
- Develop a 2×2 matrix on an area of interest and develop scenarios for changing positions
- Write a new ending for Seinfeld, CSI, M*A*S*H, Desperate Housewives, SITC… or your favorite show
- Go to an ethnic restaurant and order something you have never had before
- Go to a railroad station or airport and take the first train or plane to depart
- Imagine a world without oil, cars, telephones, internet, (fill in the blank)

1. How do you make time and space for imagination in your life and in your organization?

2. How do you encourage an imaginative mindset?

3. How do you articulate the role of imagination in your organization's goals to be innovative or creative?

4. Can you identify any initiative that has imagination at its core?

5. How do you get alignment for imaginative ideas? How do you help others see a future that is not yet here?

Wishing you the magic of imagination.

"Imagination is more Important than Knowledge."
Albert Einstein

Imagine a world where "THINKLOVE Leadership" has become the norm. To exercise your imagination, create a depiction in the space provided below that captures the essence of that world.

REFLECTION #36: BALANCING THE PAST, PRESENT, AND FUTURE

Transformational leaders enthusiastically and passionately invite their teams and their imaginations to the future while simultaneously keeping them grounded in the present and reminding them of the lessons of the past. They create a vision of future possibility and they demonstrate how today's challenges and actions will propel them to that desired future. They remind others of the company's history and tradition and use past wins and losses objectively in these conversations to underscore resiliency and evolution. They resist the temptation to become enthralled with future innovation at the cost of attending to today's needs, and they understand that the past, present, and future must be woven together for a cohesive organizational story. They hire a diverse group of people who embody enough differences in skills and perspectives to accommodate the gifts of the past, present, and future. They maintain an organizational pulse to react when the focus on today and tomorrow needs to be shifted. Visually, they keep a hand on the wheel, use the rearview mirror when appropriate, and always keep an eye on the horizon.

1. How does your vision for the future incorporate the lessons of the past?

2. Are you able to articulate the bridge between past, present, and future with enough enthusiasm and passion to make the organization's story compelling?

3. How do you use the company legacy or your personal experience to build confidence that your organization can withstand challenges and obstacles?

4. How do you keep abreast of the trends and initiatives that are driving future developments in your industry, well enough to be able to articulate the path from today to tomorrow?

5. Can you point to evidence that you are leading in a way that is "future ready" while also supporting today's excellence?

May you live comfortably in the past, present, and future.

_____

_____

_____

_____

_____

_____

_____

_____

_____

_____

_____

_____

_____

_____

_____

_____

_____

_____

_____

_____

_____

_____

_____

REFLECTION #37
FINANCIAL PERFORMANCE AND PROSPERITY

Impactful leaders embrace the fact that driving the organization's financial success is central to their job as a leader. They understand the levers of financial performance, and they are skilled at articulating how various roles contribute to financial success. They embed the conversation of financial performance in their daily leadership communications in a way that is meaningful to those they lead, with a fluidity that supports the organization's overall vision/mission. They have an authentic way of conveying that financial success also means organizational and personal achievement. These leaders underscore that financial success belongs to everyone in the organization, and they show how their employees can contribute through, for example, improving their efficiencies and operational performance, implementing best practices, and enhancing customer relationships. These leaders can tell stories that help employees relate such things as cash flows and margins to their own personal roles and lives. These leaders redefine financial success as a form of stewardship and an honorable pursuit.

1. How do you express an authentic connection to the organization's financial performance?

2. How do you explain to your team how they contribute to everyone's financial success?

3. How do you tie financial performance to the overall vision/ mission of the company?

4. How do you take swift action when your team is negatively impacting financial performance?

5. Are you in constant conversation with your fellow leaders about prosperity?

Wishing you meaningful conversations about financial performance.

_____
_____
_____
_____
_____
_____
_____
_____
_____
_____
_____
_____
_____
_____
_____
_____
_____
_____
_____
_____
_____
_____
_____

REFLECTION #38:
GROWTH AND EXPANSION

Successful leaders are passionate about taking their company and departments to broader landscapes and increasing market participation. They view the growth of their company as part of their basic mandate, and they are always in search of new and different ways to serve their customers and other stakeholders. These leaders know that highly valued employees are attracted to organizations that are growing and thriving, and these leaders view growth as a way of becoming an employer of choice. In contrast, they understand failure to grow organizational value could run the risk of losing employees, customers, and viability. They view expansion broadly and seek opportunities geographically, through related business sectors and via new ventures. They help define growth in the organization in a way that is appropriate for their circumstances. They don't rely solely on the growth plans of the past and they are comfortable taking new risks when appropriate. However, these leaders are intentional in their growth objectives and do not pursue growth for growth's sake.

1. How are you contributing to your company's growth and value?

2. Can you recognize embedded growth in your current business plan?

3. How do you communicate the growth mandate in daily conversations?

4. Are there opportunities for growth that you aren't pursuing? Why or why not?

5. How are you preparing yourself and your organization for those emerging opportunities?

Wishing you and your company continuous growth.

"Without continual growth and progress, such words as improvement and success have no meaning." Benjamin Franklin

REFLECTION #39:
ARE YOU HUNGRY?

Impactful leaders often have a hunger that pushes and propels them to do more and be more. They are never satisfied with the status quo, and they believe deep in their hearts that they always have more to give to the world. In Lencioni's book, *Humble, Hungry, and Smart*, he emphasizes that these leaders:

- do more than is required in his/her job
- have a passion for the mission of the team
- feel a personal responsibility for the overall success of the team

He underscores that this type of hunger is nested in healthy passion rather than a need based on ego, greed, or emptiness. In *Humble, Hungry, Hustle*, Brad Lomenick identifies hunger as being critical to leadership success and defines it as compilation of ambition, curiosity, passion, innovation, imagination, and bravery. Conscious leaders know the impetus behind their hunger, and they use it to sustain their enthusiasm. They demonstrate the difference between the traditional thought of being "power hungry" and the power of being a hungry leader.

1. What are you hungry for? What is driving your hunger?

2. Can you give an example of someone who is or was "power hungry?" How is that different from being a hungry leader?

3. When and how have you settled for the status quo? Why?

4. Have there been times in your life when you found yourself comfortable with the status quo even though you intuitively knew something greater was waiting?

5. Do you have a practice that fuels your hunger?

May you always strive for something more.

REFLECTION #40:
ELIMINATING THE NEED TO FIT IN

While the need for authenticity in the workplace is today's rallying cry, the risks of being authentic are still ever-present. Without doubt, we continue to be judged by the clothes we wear, the accent we speak with, our gender, the color of our skin, and our thinking process. Meetings continue to be dominated by conventional norms, and often have unwritten rules governing our manner of speaking and adherence to hierarchy. Transformational leaders have the courage to set new rules and reject the idea that the status quo must be maintained. They don't require team members to fit in or to continue with historical limits to personal expression. These leaders model "there's room for everyone at the table," and they look for and address signs that conformity is required for membership. They understand there are many subtle ways that continue to portray the need to fit in and they work to eliminate them in their company's advertisements, the office décor, the food offered, the music played, and the leadership gurus studied. These leaders work to destroy anything that impedes authenticity.

1. Where in the organization do you see signs that conformity is required?

2. Are your meetings dominated by people who dress alike, speak alike, and think alike?

3. How do you safeguard against the unwritten rules of your corporation or institutions?

4. How do you personally encourage true authenticity? How do you model it in your own life?

5. What unwritten rules exist that may discourage authenticity?

Here's to eliminating the "fitting in" requirement.

"I want to know if you are prepared to live in the world with its harsh need to change you. If you can look back with firm eyes saying this is where I stand."
David Whyte

_____

_____

_____

_____

_____

_____

_____

_____

_____

_____

_____

_____

_____

REFLECTION #41:
UNCOVERING STRENGTHS AND TALENTS

Conscious leaders see perfection within imperfection. Acknowledging genius is granted to all of us in some way but not in every way, and it lives side by side with less developed gifts. In addition, these leaders know that the brilliance that lies within each of us is often covered up by ego, fear, and past experiences, etc. With this understanding, they search for ways to draw out individual strengths and resist the urge to focus solely on what's wrong, or to dismiss people because they may be lacking in one particular area. They spend time uncovering submerged gifts and they provide opportunities for self-discovery. Conscious leaders then provide a platform to demonstrate these talents in a way that builds confidence and eagerness to grow. These leaders have a mission to nurture the gifts of others, and they create a culture where appreciation of different ways of manifesting genius is the norm. These leaders understand Einstein's message, "Everyone is a genius, but if you judge a fish on its ability to climb a tree, it will live its whole life believing that it's stupid."

1. How do uncover the strengths and talents of your team members?

2. How do you handle it when you are faced with a weakness that conflicts with what you value most at work?

3. How can you put the puzzle together powerfully by combining strengths and weaknesses of your team in a conscious way?

4. Do you spend more time trying to fix what is wrong or shining a light on what is working for your team members?

5. How can you stand in the middle of this messy and imperfect world and still lead with power and purpose?

Wishing you the vision to see perfection in imperfection.

"A leader is one who... Has more faith in people than they do, and . . . who holds opportunities open long enough for their competence to re-emerge."
Margaret J. Wheatley

Reflection #42: Leadership Is a Conversation

Transformational leaders embrace the idea that "leadership is a conversation" (Groysberg and Slind, 2012), and for the conversation to be effective, it must be:

1. Intentional—purposeful and driven while building alignment with the organization's objectives.
2. Intimate—minimizing the distance between leaders and their employees to seek and earn trust.
3. Interactive—open and fluid dialogue promotes employee support to speak up.
4. Inclusive—allowing employees to expand their roles and participate in the makeup of an organization's story.

Transformational leaders plan these conversations as part of their daily assignments and manage them like any other part of their business plan. They invite everyone to the conversation regardless of status. They also provide a platform for give and take and create a safe space for that platform. They practice and improve their conversation management skills year after year, and they create alignment around the elements of conversational leadership. These leaders teach their fellow leaders how to embrace conversation as a leadership art form, and they are intentional in their approach. They notice the prominent organizational conversation day by day.

1. How are you being intentional in your leadership conversations today?

2. How would you define the quality of conversation you are having?

3. Who is prominently at the table? How are you inviting people into the conversation?

4. What ensures the conversations are interactive?

5. How do you create the intimacy for real conversations?

May your conversations be real and powerful.

_____

_____

_____

_____

_____

_____

_____

_____

_____

_____

_____

_____

_____

_____

_____

_____

_____

_____

_____

_____

REFLECTION #43:
RECOGNIZING MASKS

Inspirational leaders recognize that while masks in the workplace are common, they undermine trust and limit creativity and performance. They believe that recognizing and honoring the uniqueness of each individual is key to employee engagement and development. These leaders model the practice of discovering and removing their own masks, and they reveal who they are with naked courage. They continuously mine for the truth about themselves and their employees, and they create a culture of safety for mask removal. They reward both this authenticity and honor the ultimate face that emerges. These leaders also know that asking people to "remove their masks" might be language that is not understood, and they use words that can be heard by their teams. For example, the questions, "Where are we pretending?" and "What conversations are we avoiding?" may help the organization address any unspoken problems or cover-ups. Conscious leaders know the ultimate question is "Why do they or anyone they lead feel the need to wear a mask?"

1. Do you wear a mask from time to time? How does it serve you? Can you give it a name?

2. Have you uncovered why you started wearing it? What is the story you have told yourself?

3. What fears do you need to face and overcome to show up as the "real you?" How can you model that for employees?

4. How do you explain what it means to wear a mask and how do you create a safe space for employees to share who they really are?

5. How do you help create a culture that supports this type of reflection? How do you describe the danger of wearing a mask every day?

Wishing you a lifetime of discovering the true shape of your own face.

"Wearing a mask wears you out. Faking it is fatiguing. The most exhausting activity is pretending to be what you know you aren't."
Rick Warren

REFLECTION #44:
BELIEVING IN POSSIBILITY

Remarkable leaders often have an optimism that is supported by realism. They don't live in a fantasy world—they see things exactly as they are and still know that possibilities are limitless. These leaders infuse the organization with their firm belief in possibility, and as a result, employees rise to the organization's challenges in a more confident way. When their team members are tempted to slide into an unproductive state, these leaders are skilled at navigating those team members to a place of hopefulness and focus. These leaders ground their optimism in a language and reality employees can buy into. These leaders have an energy of optimism that maintains organizational flow despite market upsets, operational setbacks, and strategic missteps. As a result, the organization responds with a sense of power and confidence.

1. How would you describe your ability to remain optimistic in the face of negative evidence?

2. How does your language demonstrate your optimism about the future?

3. What is your optimism based on? How do you practice mining for possibility? What role does your intuition play?

4. How do you keep your organization open to new and unexpected possibilities?

5. How do you infuse the organization with optimism and possibility when you are not meeting your goals, when the market has turned against you, when your company is being acquired, etc.?

Wishing you a world of possibilities.

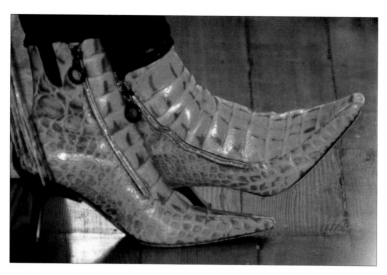

"You had the Power all along my dear."
Glenda the Good Witch

REFLECTION # 45:
LETTING GO

Transformational leaders know that all things change—and that the traits, behaviors, thoughts, and practices that served us well yesterday must constantly be reevaluated. These leaders embrace the idea that we should practice the art of letting go of what is no longer effective. This letting go could include a release of control, the past, previous hurts, known practices, and ways of working. In 2015, Fast Company identified "letting go" as the leadership trait of the future. Leaders who let go can point to evidence that they have evolved to meet the needs of their businesses and people over time. They are open to the advice of others and utilize self-exploration to look for signs that they are stuck. These leaders understand that you must let go of the rope you're holding to catch a new one, and they admit when they might still be holding on. These leaders know that releasing creates space for new ideas and opportunities.

1. Do you have a self-evaluation process that examines whether there are practices or thoughts that are no longer serving you?

2. Are you discovering things in your life that are operating as roadblocks that you need to release?

3. Do you have a practice of release that helps you let go of past experiences or past habits?

4. How do you enlist the help of others to identify when you are stuck?

5. How do you build practices in your organization that achieves the same release result?

Wishing you leadership of change, release, and evolution.

"Let me fall if I must fall. The one I become will catch me."
Sheryl Sandberg

_____
_____
_____
_____
_____
_____
_____
_____
_____
_____
_____
_____
_____
_____

REFLECTION #46:
USING VOICE

Mindful leaders understand the attribute of "voice," and acknowledge that it encompasses everything you communicate to yourself and to the world. These leaders accept that this voice is presented through a filter that incorporates all our beliefs and past experiences, and they work to unravel those filters. These leaders know that any voice can be powerful and authentic or anemic and impotent. They pay attention to how they use their own voice, and they coach others about showing up and using their unique voices. Leaders develop and manage their own voice while simultaneously facilitating opportunity and equality in the workplace. They're conscious of whether they overuse their voice or shy away from using it. These leaders recognize that certain members of the team may be more hesitant to use their voices, and are cognizant of the impact of gender and culture. They make sure the microphone is shared with diverse people, to avoid a skewed organizational voice representing only a particular communication type. Conscious leaders revel when new and provocative voices are added to the organization.

1. What does the concept of "voice" mean to you?

2. How are you mindful, intentional, and conscious with your own powerful voice?

3. Who or what is the prominent voice of your organization right now? What is its main message?

4. Are you often misunderstood, or can you easily speak with clarity and conviction?

5. How do you manage voices within the organization ensuring that team members have an equal opportunity for expression?

Wishing you the wisdom of the individual and collective voice.

Inspirational leaders know that good humor is an effective tool for transformation. These leaders understand that while the work they do is meaningful and serious, bringing fun and playfulness to this work expands its accessibility to the world. They laugh at themselves, seek joy in the workplace, and approach the various mountains and plateaus of life with a light-hearted confidence. These leaders know that humor is a strong tool in their toolbox that can sometimes reach in and connect when all else has failed. They know laughter is uplifting and contagious, and don't view laughter as a sign of nonproductivity. It has been shown that people who take themselves too seriously are, ironically, not taken serious by their peers. The value of humor and laugher in the workplace was detailed by Jacqueline Smith in a Forbes article titled "10 Reasons Why Humor Is A Key To Success At Work" (Smith, 2013). In that article she identified many ways that laughter increases productivity, stating, "Humor creates an upbeat atmosphere that encourages integration, brainstorming of new ideas, and the feeling that there are few risks in thinking outside the box." She also noted the following benefits:

1. Humor is a stress buster
2. Humor is humanizing
3. Humor builds trust
4. Humor boasts morale

1. Where does humor and laughter show up in your work life?

2. Can you laugh at yourself and truly feel comfortable in that moment?

3. How do you show your team that although their work is serious, it is compatible with fun in the workplace?

4. When was the last time you had a good laugh with your team?

5. How can you be more intentional with bringing good humor to work?

Wishing you a day full of laughter.

_____

_____

_____

_____

_____

_____

_____

"The most wasted of days is the one without laughter."
EE Cummings

REFLECTION #48:
INCORPORATING THE EXTERNAL WORLD

Insightful leaders are skilled at balancing internal concerns with external realities. They orchestrate a richer organizational conversation by injecting "what's going on in the world" messages into the day-to-day operational improvement topics. These leaders are conscious that organizations do not exist in a vacuum but operate within the context of global and local impacts. These leaders provide personal insights and facilitate interaction with people outside their industry and geographical domain to prevent insular and parochial viewpoints. These leaders understand that learning is expanded through external information and a diversity of experiences, and they invest in their people to make sure they have those experiences. These leaders are on the lookout for insular thinking and they recognize the global impacts on every business.

1. What percentage of your meetings are dedicated to external updates?

2. How do you contribute to bringing the external and internal worlds together?

3. How can you invite your team into a broader conversation about the world in a creative and energized way?

4. How do you personally resist the temptation to get mired in "internalities?"

5. What education, association, or experience do you need to be a leader who brings the world to your people?

Wishing you a global perspective.

REFLECTION #49:
SPEAKING TRUTH TO SELF

Mindful leaders accept that the most courageous conversation is the ongoing one we have with self. These leaders know that leadership growth and evolution require them to stay connected to the brutal and beautiful truth of who we are and how we show up in the world. They embed a truth-telling practice in their lives, looking into their own hearts and minds as an integral part of their individual performance improvement. They utilize a variety of tools, including meditation, journaling, counseling, educational classes, and other seminars. They don't look for reassurance during these practices, they look for revelation. These mindful leaders also know that self-exploration doesn't happen by chance or on its own, and they reserve a few minutes each day to stay connected to self. They understand that deeper self-inquiry is an important part of being a stable and engaging leader.

1. What is your practice for being honest with yourself regarding your feelings, your relationships, and your ambitions?

2. Can you see a link between your leadership consciousness and organizational performance? How does one impact the other?

3. Can you see the connection between your ability to speak truth to self and your competency to speak truth to those you lead?

4. Can you be brutally and beautifully honest? Can you maintain self-love and acceptance in your inquiry?

5. What are three messages that your inner voice wants to share with you today?

Wishing you a day full of truth and growth.

"Yesterday I was clever, so I wanted to change the world.
Today I am wise, so I am changing myself."
Rumi

_____

_____

_____

_____

_____

_____

_____

_____

_____

_____

REFLECTION #50:
POWER AND MINDFULNESS

Mindful leaders who activate their true power listen to themselves, to those they lead, and to the world at large in order to move beyond traditional expressions of power. They understand that this listening is not accomplished through hearing alone but extends to their whole selves—incorporating all input and evidence available. These leaders intrinsically know mindfulness plays an important role in facilitating the leader's ability to do that, since mindfulness at its core is the ability to stay in the present moment. Without the ability to be truly present, leaders miss subtle cues from themselves and from the world. To access and activate their true power, mindful leaders are willing to devote the time and space to look below the surface and sit with the questions a deep listening and presence provokes. They are open to feeling the discomfort of the process and find a way to move through any self-limiting actions and beliefs.

During the past fifty days, have you developed a keener sense of the type of power and mindfulness you want to bring to your leadership? What have the you heard in these reflections that resonated with you in a way that will mold your leadership expression? What have you heard from others that lets you know that your work is being impactful? How do you use that feedback to make the next fifty days even more meaningful?

1. What have you heard these past fifty days that has significantly influenced your belief about leadership?

2. How has improved listening and mindfulness enhanced your leadership capabilities?

3. What concepts or behaviors are you still struggling to understand or implement? How can you address any gaps?

4. How are you sharing information with your teams?

5. What are your goals for the next 50 days?

Wishing you the power of presence.

_____

_____

_____

_____

_____

_____

_____

_____

_____

_____

_____

_____

_____

_____

_____

_____

_____

_____

_____

REFLECTION #51:
SWEAT THE SMALL STUFF

Conscious leaders know that how you do anything is how you do everything, and they focus on today's "small stuff" to drive more significant behaviors and the overall corporate culture. These leaders pay attention to the little things that happen every day, and they practice the presence required to really see them. These leaders pay attention to subtle evidence that points to where their employees are mentally and emotionally, and they accept it's the day-to-day actions that shine the truth on corporate values and culture. They understand that if small actions are out of alignment with stated values, the larger vision is completely out of reach. Impactful leaders do not wait until the minor indicators evolve into larger issues, but rather they address the problems in the moment and institute action for sustainable change. This attention to detail is equally important in customer interactions, as Roy Sutherland underlined in his popular Ted Talk where he urges us to pay attention to the small stuff: https://www.ted.com/talks/rory_sutherland_sweat_the_small_stuff

1. Are there any small things today that are signaling that you or your employees do not embrace the corporate values or priorities completely?

2. What are some small current behaviors—both positive and negative—that are shining a light on company values?

3. How do you draw daily attention to detail?

4. How do you communicate the idea that how you do anything is how you do everything?

5. How do you model a "sweat the small stuff" leadership philosophy?

Wishing you a day filled with small insights.

"It's the little things that make the big things possible. Only close attention to the fine details of any operation makes the operation first class."

J. Willard Marriott

REFLECTION #52:
CELEBRATE DIVERSITY

To perhaps state the obvious, transformational leaders know that organizations thrive when diversity is welcomed and promoted. These leaders understand that as the world changes, the beliefs and practices that formed the foundation of their industries and companies must also change. To facilitate and utilize new thinking and new perspectives, mindful leaders seek out people who have experiences and backgrounds different from their own, and encourage their colleagues to do the same. They are alert to their self-tendency to attach themselves to others who mirror them. These leaders know that you can't fake appreciating differences, and they know the greatest respect is to grant equality day in and day out. They find new ways to celebrate these differences and ensure everyone is accepted and valued for their unique style, voice, and contribution. More important, they own and talk about this important topic.

1. How do you promote diversity? How comfortable are you leading this promotion?

2. What can you point to that shows how much you value diversity? How has your perspective changed over time?

3. Where in your organization is diversity lacking? What are you doing to help fill in the gaps?

4. Have your life experiences prepared you to accept and celebrate people from different cultures and points of view?

5. How do you address negative connotations related to diversity efforts?

Wishing you the benefits of diversity.

"We all should know that diversity makes for a rich tapestry, and we must understand that all the threads of the tapestry are equal in value no matter what their color."

Maya Angelou

REFLECTION #53:
MANAGE ARROGANCE AND INSECURITY

Mindful leaders are on a continual journey of personal growth and self-discovery. They acknowledge the tendency to question both self-worth and competency, while at other times exaggerating both. Acknowledging that tension, these leaders search for a self-view and self-expression that is neither arrogant nor self-depreciating. Bestselling author and researcher Brené Brown coined the phrase, "Don't shrink back. Don't puff up. Stand on your sacred ground." Puffing, standing, and shrinking can show up in different ways depending on your consciousness, but it can always jeopardize personal power. The key is to be mindful of your inner feelings and note what is showing up for you. The "sacred ground" Brené Brown refers to is your true power source—where your free spirit, intuition, and courage combine to provide a firm foundation for leadership. It is a place where you can be strong enough to ignore peer pressure or cultural self-story that undermines your true place in the world. These leaders aren't trying to stand out or fit in; they consistently exhibit self-confidence with humility. As David Whyte so poetically reminds us, "Standing on solid ground is the greatest achievement."

1. What limits your unique self-expression?

2. Can you think of examples where you have found yourself either "shrinking" or "puffing up?"

3. Do you have other experiences where other leaders displayed superiority or inferiority?

4. Why do you think leaders may display or feel the extremes of arrogance and insecurity?

5. How could you expand your ability to stand stronger in your own story?

Wishing you the strength to build your own solid ground.

_____

_____

_____

_____

_____

_____

_____

_____

_____

_____

_____

_____

"Don't Puff Up, Don't Shrink back, Stand on sacred ground."
Brené Brown

REFLECTION #54:
ATTRACT THE BEST AND BRIGHTEST

Breakthrough leaders are on a continuous search for top talent to join their teams, and they create a workplace that beckons that talent. To support the talent search, they communicate a vision of employment that is challenging, exciting, and meaningful. Their organizations, large or small, are known for attracting and retaining the best and the brightest, and they consistently redefine what it means to be best and brightest in order to meet their business goals and culture objectives. As a result, they create a culture of diversity, excellence, and growth. Once hired, these best and brightest employees benefit from leaders who know how to build the required relationships to engage with these employees and bring out their greatest assets. These leaders accept that the organization is only as good as the people they hire, grow, and support. They spend time in interviews and understanding recruiting philosophy and methodology. These mindful leaders are involved in selecting new members to the team and they know that culture fit is included in the definition of best and brightest.

1. How would you describe your organization's recruiting methodology and success?

2. How do you describe the best and brightest? Do you include psychometrics or other methods to determine organizational fit?

3. What role do you personally play in attracting the best and the brightest?

4. How does your marketing beckon the talent of the future?

5. How has your organization's tactics changed over time to attract the freshest talent?

Wishing you a career surrounded by the best and the brightest.

REFLECTION #55:
BEING HUMAN

Conscious leaders understand that leadership encompasses all their humanness—their weaknesses, strengths, their darkness and their light, their victories and their wounds, as well as all circumstances they have experienced to date. Consequently, they acknowledge that their leadership cannot be separated from who they are as human beings and all the events and encounters that led them to this moment. These experiences can be dramatic or subtle, but the negative ones can often be characterized as an abrasion, bruise, or trauma—in other words, a wound. These leaders realize that they can use the knowledge gained from a wounding event and the resilience earned from it, and they purposely incorporate those lessons into their leadership. These leaders are continuously looking for ways to convert past pain into present positive energy, in order to help create a better workplace and a better world. Mark Nepo explores this concept in the poem below:

It is said that soul's intent on Living
Will reach deep into their wounds
And bring out the fire living there
Which out in the open
Will Turn to Comforting Light
It is said that those intent on making things better
Will Reach deep into their minds
And Bring out the Fire there
Which out in the open
Turns only to obvious truth

1. Can you identify any past negative experiences that have affected your leadership?

2. What past hurts may you still be holding on to?

3. How comfortable are you being human in the workplace? How do you display it?

4. What past lessons have strengthened your leadership?

5. When you reach deep into your mind and heart, what fire is there waiting to be transformed into truth?

Wishing you the ability to be fully human.

_____

_____

_____

_____

_____

_____

*"You are the hero of your own story. The privilege of a
lifetime is being who you are." Joseph Campbell*

REFLECTION #56:
BRING STRATEGY TO LIFE

Successful leaders accept that one of their primary jobs is to bring strategy to life for members of their teams. They spend time in external and internal conversations about the company's strategy, and they dedicate time with their teams to discuss where the organization is going and why. They have a keen ability to communicate a strategy with clarity and passion and to inspire employees to want to understand it. These leaders are great storytellers and they weave strategic questions through dialogue and meetings and build strategic competence throughout the organization. These leaders continuously invite employees at all levels to participate in the ongoing discussion and choices of strategy and they are excited about bringing their strategy to life and to fruition. These mindful leaders breathe life into the strategic discussion.

1. Can you discuss your organization's strategy in three minutes or less?

2. How emotionally attached are you to the organization's strategic direction? Are you authentically excited?

3. How do you invite employees into the strategy conversation? How do you influence the conversation?

4. What are the key strategic choices you are making now? How do you use storytelling to bring them alive?

5. Do employees understand the company's direction and why? How do you know?

Wishing you a day of strategic clarity and excitement.

REFLECTION #57:
RECOGNITION AND CELEBRATION

Effective leaders understand the role of recognition and celebration in performance improvement and achievement. They make the time to notice, appreciate, and acknowledge the smaller achievements in the organization as well as the larger wins. They understand the connection to appreciation and creating trust in the workplace, and they spend time in authentic and generous recognition. These leaders also know that meaningless fanfare does not substitute for authentic acknowledgment of a job well done, and they are purposeful in their use of celebration. Effective leaders make sure they don't overuse or underuse the strategic imperative of celebration, and they work with their teams to embed the substantive meaning of these events.

1. How you use recognition and celebration as a leadership tool?

2. Do you embed the practice of recognition celebration into your business plan and budget?

3. How do you ensure that these acknowledgments are authentic and meaningful rather than "fluff and puff?"

4. How do you personally make the time to offer gratitude and appreciation?

5. How does your organizational culture impact the nature of your recognition celebrations?

Wishing you meaningful reasons to celebrate.

"The more you celebrate your life the more there is in life to celebrate. "
Oprah Winfrey

_____

_____

_____

_____

_____

_____

_____

_____

_____

_____

_____

_____

_____

_____

_____

_____

REFLECTION #58:
MANAGING LEADERSHIP TRANSITION

Mindful leaders know that effectively managing leadership transitions is vitally important for organizational growth and continuity. Accordingly, these leaders assemble a strong team that is prepared to respond to employee anxiety, fear, or frustration during leadership transitions, and they incorporate leadership transitions into their strategic planning. They have established effective succession plans and assembled strong teams to manage agreed-upon personnel transition strategies. However, when they are the departing leader, they ensure there is a proper closing with their teams and the organization. They also recognize that succession plans are needed throughout all levels of the organizations and not simply at the executive level. These conscious leaders also create a culture that can survive leadership changes and other transitions because the organization is prepared both structurally and emotionally. Conscious leaders create sufficient individual confidence and passion to ensure self-sustaining momentum and to prevent dependence on any particular leader, and they resist the urge to idolize or demonize any past leaders.

1. Does your organization have a formal succession plan and process?

2. What went well? What could have been done differently?

3. How do you make sure there is no gap between the new and the previous leader?

4. How have you personally closed well throughout your career when you left a company or department?

5. What is the most successful transition you have witnessed? Why did it work well?

Wishing you many successful transitions during your lifetime.

REFLECTION #59:
REVOLUTIONARY MINDSET

Courageous leaders accept that certain situations must be met with a revolutionary mindset. Depending on the situation, it could require the sale of a company or the dismantling of an entire structure or a department. This mindset is appropriate when nothing less than destruction and restoration will do.

Revolutionary leaders accept the truth that this type of transformation pushes many people outside of their comfort zones and often results in conflict. They approach this conflict and accept its necessity from a healthy perspective with both empathy and resolve. These leaders move through the revolution knowing that the members of their teams are stronger than they know, and provide unwavering support to each individual to move through obstacles and challenges. Revolutionary leaders don't back down, knowing that the greater good must be achieved. Rather, these leaders always stand in strength and love, and do revolution differently. They never try to maintain the current structure in the name of comfort, and they are constantly evaluating whether incremental changes are enough.

1. How does the term "revolutionary leader" make you feel? Does it sound honorable or heartless?

2. Can you describe a time that you could have been characterized as "revolutionary?"

3. Can you authentically say you believe the people who comprise your teams are strong enough for revolutionary change?

4. If you were called upon to lead a revolutionary change, how would you approach it?

5. What is your current role in leading a transformational revolution for your division or company?

Wishing you a revolution you can stand behind.

_____

_____

_____

_____

_____

_____

_____

_____

"You don't make progress by standing on the sidelines, whimpering and complaining. You make progress by implementing ideas." Shirley Chisholm

Transformational leaders can stamp a deeper meaning on achievements—acknowledging not just the actions of their employees but the purpose behind those actions. These leaders remind us of the "why" that underpins plans and strategies. While they insist that progress is measured in a quantifiable way, transformational leaders also articulate the story surrounding goals and objectives. In his book *Start with Why*, Simon Sinek states, "Why is our purpose, cause, or belief that inspires us to do what we do." Through his research on leaders who have had the greatest influence in the world, he discovered that these leaders think, act, and communicate differently than other leaders. He highlights that companies which start with "why" are more innovative, influential, and profitable than others. Likewise, leaders who inspire us at the deepest level never let us forget the reasons we do what we do. They know that promoting purpose and meaning in the workplace is central to a leadership role.

The Golden Circle
Simon Sinek

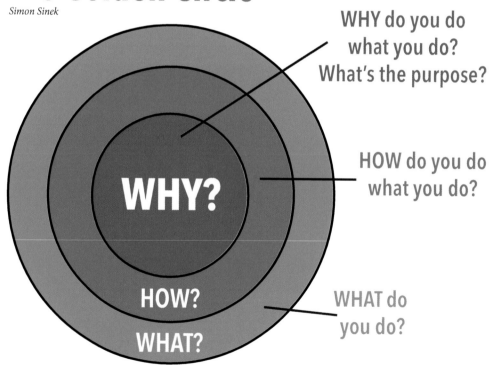

WHY do you do what you do? What's the purpose?

HOW do you do what you do?

WHAT do you do?

WHY?

HOW?

WHAT?

1. Do you articulate the "why" of your company? How skilled are you at weaving the why story with the quantifiable data?

2. Which story are you more comfortable telling? Who do you know that is really skilled at articulating both?

3. How do you tell your personal "why" for your actions?

4. How do you facilitate the process for employees to discover their own "why" of work?

5. How do you build cohesiveness among the why and the how?

Wishing you a day full of meaningful "why" conversations.

REFLECTION #61:
LEADERSHIP CONSCIOUSNESS

Mindful leaders accept that the organizations they lead are limited by the level of leadership consciousness embedded in the organization, and they view building their own personal consciousness as one of their key objectives. We define consciousness as being aware of the world and one's surroundings, and being mindful in the execution of our leadership. These leaders are seekers; they spend time in self-discovery and they create platforms for their team members to engage in meaningful internal dialogue. Inspirational leaders understand Albert Einstein's quote, "No problem can be solved by the same level of consciousness that created it," and they build their work conversations around this adage. They can explain to their teams what the term "consciousness" means to them and they search for ways to make the term accessible to the teams they lead.

1. What does the word "consciousness" mean to you?

2. Can you point to evidence that your own consciousness has expanded over the years?

3. How do you build room for discussions that engage employees in a way that broadens their thinking?

4. How can you build your awareness and mindfulness to benefit your organization?

5. How would you describe the practices within your organization that impede or promote consciousness and mindfulness?

Wishing you continuous awakening.

"If you cannot find a group whose consciousness matches your own, be the source of one. Others of like consciousness will be drawn to you." Neale Donald Walsch

_____

_____

_____

_____

_____

_____

_____

_____

_____

_____

_____

_____

_____

_____

_____

REFLECTION #62:
CHALLENGE BUREAUCRACY

When German political economist Max Weber first devised the bureaucratic theory of management in the late nineteenth century, his intention was to combat the nepotism and unproductiveness rife in the family-run businesses of the day. Weber believed that efficient organizations needed to "have a strict hierarchy or authority, clear rules and regulations, standardized procedures, and meticulous record keeping" (*Momentum: How to Build it, Keep it, or Get it Back*, McQueen, 2016). Ironically, the very organizational approach that set out to drive efficiency has, over time, resulted in the opposite outcome.

Bureaucracy has been noted to exist not only in Fortune 500 companies but also creep into small startups and midsize organizations. Signs of bureaucracy include needless and outdated polices, endless paperwork, and the requirement of useless approvals. Often thwarting innovation and ownership, these systems are designed to support hierarchy and control.

Rather than ignore or simply complain about impediments embedded in hierarchy and bureaucracy, transformational leaders challenge these systems and offer new ways of thinking to minimize their impact. These leaders have the confidence and skill to influence at varying levels of the organization. They use this ability to facilitate less reliance on rules and regulations, and greater focus on employee empowerment.

1. How would you describe the level of bureaucracy in your organization?

2. What are the visible and invisible signs of this bureaucratic system?

3. How are you keeping it in place or dismantling it?

4. What are some alternatives that you have used or are aware of?

5. How do you think a transition from bureaucracy to an adhocracy paradigm (defined as a flexible, adaptable, and informal organization) can occur?

Wishing you resolve to eliminate needless bureaucracy.

REFLECTION #63:
DREAM BIGGER

Optimistic leaders understand that substantial change often comes from the ability to "dream bigger." These leaders are genuinely excited about possibilities and evolution, and their enthusiasm about the future propels their teams forward into the land of tomorrow. They continually check their own mindset for self-limiting beliefs, and they are on the lookout for any thinking that restricts them. They remember the roles of imagination and curiosity, and they continually stoke both for the "dream bigger" goal. Transformational leaders are partners with their team members in the pursuit of this mind-expansion, and they understand it is a central duty of their leadership role. They reward and acknowledge the big dreamers of their organization, and they create structures to move the dreams into reality. These "dreaming bigger" leaders also model this thought practice in their own lives, and they are proud of the accomplishments made under this expansive banner.

1. How would you describe your own ability to "dream bigger?" What are some of your current visions?

2. What experiences in your past may help or hinder your ability to think expansively?

3. Would your team describe you as visionary? Why or why not?

4. What elements of your language and your meetings help in the goal of expanding minds?

5. How do you analyze the ability of your team members to think beyond what is known? How can you help expand this ability?

Wishing you an expanded mind and landscape.

"If Your Dreams don't scare you, they are too small."
Richard Branson

REFLECTION #64:
DANCE WITH AMBIGUITY

Remarkable leaders have accepted that thriving in ambiguity is a leadership imperative in today's world of rapid change and disrupted hierarchy. These leaders have learned to dance with ambiguity by resisting the urge to control everything, and through learning to act without the complete picture. They do not become overwhelmed and more dependent on facts and statistics in the current world of unlimited data. Instead, they execute decisions in confidence and do not become paralyzed by the sheer amount of information. They also understand that in this complex, ambiguous world, some of the decisions they make will be wrong, and they maintain their certainty and power in the face of that reality. Mindful leaders can model comfort amid uncertainty, and their teams grow stronger because of their ability to move forward in a flexible, agile way. These leaders and their teams strive for clarity, but they don't fear ambiguity.

1. Name decisions you have made within an ambiguous context.

2. How do you help develop an organizational mindset that deals effectively with ambiguity?

3. How do you seek more and varying viewpoints in response to growing uncertainty? How do you avoid the tendency to seek more and more information? What is the difference between those reactions?

4. How do you resist the tendency to delay decisions, but exert control in ambiguity?

5. How has your risk appetite changed over the years? Are you dancing more comfortably with ambiguity, or have you become more rigid?

May you always move forward.

_____

_____

_____

_____

_____

_____

_____

_____

_____

_____

_____

_____

"Life is about not knowing … taking the moment and making the best of it without knowing what is going to happen next." Gilda Radnor

REFLECTION #65:
VALUES IN ACTION

Trusted leaders understand that the articulation of the organization's values can be unifying and transformational, or hollow and meaningless. Accordingly, they spend a great deal of time uncovering and having the organization align on the articulation of these values. These leaders know it is the character of their people that determines the overall integrity of the organization and whether those values are lived in practice. Trusted leaders pay close attention to a "value match" when they hire, and they call forth the behaviors associated with the stated values in their daily language and actions. These leaders know that company values must also be supported by organizational structure and processes. These mindful leaders ensure that they include behaviors as part of performance management programs. They respect that values are a defining part of the organization, and they model these values in their leadership while striving to keep them embedded in the organizational conversation.

1. How do you determine if there is a "value match" when you interview potential employees?

2. How prevalent and known are your organization's values to your current employees? How do you ensure that these values are put into action?

3. How do the organization's values show up in your personal life?

4. How would you describe the "character" of your organization to a stranger?

5. How are you leading the call to keep your values meaningful?

Wishing you a day of experiencing values in action.

The business of managing performance has been under fire in recent years for being ineffective, if not a total waste of time. In fact, it has been found that the traditional approach of establishing goals at the beginning of the year and meeting once or more to review progress against those goals does not manage performance but thwarts a more creative approach, since it creates the appearance of an effective performance management system. This long-practiced approach, which limits performance management to an appraisal system, has been determined to cast too narrow a net for truly evaluating performance. Further, this one-size-fits-all mentality does not accommodate the diverse contributions of employees in the ever-changing marketplace and should not be the sole determinant of financial rewards.

It is estimated that half of the Fortune 500 companies have or soon will have removed the traditional ranking system. Some of the new systems have no annual reviews, cascading objectives, or 360-degree feedback tools. These new systems will include informal conversations contemporaneous with actions, and other mechanisms for collectively reliable performance data. One innovative solution is a mobile app for daily feedback. Organizations that do power differently strive for a one-size-fits-one approach, and continue to evaluate the effectiveness of their methodology systems. However, despite the imperfection of the current methodology, they hold people accountable for fulfilling their performance management responsibilities, and they take their own evaluations seriously. These mindful leaders don't just go through the motions but engage in an intimate, meaningful conversation.

1. What is your current performance management system? What feedback have you received about it?

2. Do you feel the current system is meaningful and effective in accomplishing your objectives? Why or why not?

3. How much time do you spend in informal discussion about

employee aspirations, goals, strengths, and weaknesses? Do you believe the frequency is adequate?

4. What new innovative approaches have you considered? How would your culture accommodate new approaches? Are there any roadblocks?

5. How does your current performance management system impact compensation today? Is it fairly administrated?

Wishing you effective performance conversations.

_____

_____

_____

_____

_____

_____

_____

_____

_____

_____

_____

_____

_____

_____

REFLECTION #67: EMBRACING INCLUSION

While closely related to diversity, inclusion incorporates the notion of belonging and an invitation to fully participate. It encourages people to feel safe, welcomed, and free to be exactly who they are. A commitment to inclusion goes beyond hiring diverse people of varying race, gender, sexual orientation, and national origin, and extends to bringing them completely and wholeheartedly into the work environment.

As early as 2012, in her book *Inclusion: The New Competitive Business Advantage*, Shirley Engelmeier noted that inclusion is a call to action within the workforce that involves employee ideas, approaches, perspectives, and personalities. She emphasizes that there is a real competitive advantage to mining and using these diverse thoughts. To be able to fully include diverse employees, the leader must be aware of any unconscious bias that often unknowingly permeates organizations and results in subtle discrimination.

To move beyond standalone diversity initiatives to an inclusive culture, we must remove traditional roadblocks such as limiting job descriptions, outdated employee assessments and human resource policies, and unchecked hiring practices. Leaders who promote an inclusion culture challenge stereotypes and watch out for practices of "mirroracracy." They provide education to managers and leaders that highlight how to create an inclusive culture and encourage employees to challenge collusive behavior such as remaining silent in the face of prejudice.

1. How would you articulate the difference between diversity and inclusion in your own words?

2. Is your organization having a broader conversation about inclusion?

3. What training is provided by your company for those who lead people and the organization as a whole?

4. How do you guard against and expose unconscious bias?

5. How do you create a sense of responsibility at all levels of the organization for inclusion, and facilitate the psychological safety to speak up?

Wishing you an open mind and inclusive heart.

_____

_____

_____

_____

_____

_____

_____

_____

_____

_____

"Diversity is being invited to the party. Inclusion is being asked to dance."
Verna Meyers

Reflection #68:
Great Leaders Produce Leaders

Good leaders and great leaders can be distinguished by several characteristics, but the most significant is whether or not they have created other leaders. Great leaders are not focused on developing followers; they are searching for partners, and they demonstrate sincere respect for the people they lead. These leaders create a culture of leadership, and they extend the leadership context to members throughout the organization. They emphasize that leadership happens at all levels, and they resist the urge to associate leadership solely with a title. They can see who and what employees might be in the future, and they offer training to accelerate their paths. They coach and mentor other potential leaders with a commitment to encourage personal growth, and they give assignments with development in mind. They never inject artificial limits to what employees can accomplish. They are proud to produce leaders.

1. How do you demonstrate respect for the members of your team? How do you make that respect intimate and individual?

2. What is your current practice for mentoring, coaching, and developing?

3. Name three leaders you have produced. How have they made you proud?

4. How have you created a culture of leadership? Who is a leader that doesn't have a title but that you recognize as a leader?

5. How do you offer roles and training to accelerate leadership growth?

Wishing you future leaders you are proud of.

REFLECTION #69:
THE ART OF STORYTELLING

One of the leadership traits often overlooked is the art of storytelling. As Bill Gurley of Benchmark sums it up, "The great storytellers have an unfair competitive advantage. They are going to recruit better, they will be darlings in the press, they are going to raise money more easily and at higher prices, they are going to close amazing business developer partnerships, and they are going to have a strong and cohesive corporate culture. Perhaps more to the point, they are more likely to deliver a positive investment return" (Gurley, 2015).

In addition, mindful leaders expand the goal of storytelling by inspiring others to want to be part of the story. They have a skill and a passion for creating a vision for a future that everyone wants to step into, and they detail a path for broad participation. These leaders know the effect of storytelling can be broad and help deal with conflict, let go of the past, and embrace change and future possibilities. Through their stories, they help people cope with fear, uncertainty, and doubt.

Telling a story provides a way for leaders to connect with others, and offers a natural way to form trust. When leaders tell the most important story of all—their own personal story—they open a space for others to tell theirs, and together these collective stories create a more intimate work community. Personal stories shared by leaders help to embed storytelling into the organizational culture.

1. How have you used storytelling at work?

2. What story have you heard someone else share that had a profound impact on you?

3. What skills do you need to enhance your effectiveness as a storyteller?

4. What life experience or personal story can you share that reveals

a lesson you have learned?

5. How can you encourage storytelling as part of your organizational culture?

May your storytelling inspire you and those you lead.

_____

_____

_____

_____

_____

_____

_____

"We live in a time where each of us will be asked to reach deeper, speak more bravely, live more from the fierce perspectives of the poetic imagination."
David Whyte

REFLECTION #70:
OPEN LEARNER

Abraham Lincoln famously said, "The dogmas of the quiet past are insufficient for our stormy future." These words rang true in 1864, and they are just as relevant today. Notwithstanding that truth, leaders are often tempted to hold on to the quiet past. Mindful leaders learn the art of "emptying the mind" and allowing space for new thoughts and ideas, even about their most deeply held beliefs and firmly rooted practices. These leaders resist the urge to rely on expert status because they know they can learn from a variety of people and experiences. They also understand that the organization's ability to produce "open learners" is largely dependent on their own ability to be one. These leaders exude excitement about learning new things and revisiting old conclusions.

Christina Lattimer's article "Five Characteristics of an Open-Minded Leader" (Peopledevelopmentmagazine.com, 2013), highlighted that an open-minded leader has:

1. A thrust for learning
2. Curiosity
3. The ability to see things easily from different perspectives
4. An acceptance and respect for others' beliefs and choices
5. An awareness that their own and others' beliefs and fillers can be limited

These leaders are actually more decisive because they have considered diverse views and perspectives in their decision making.

1. What practices do you use to "empty the mind?"

2. Can you identify any beliefs or fillers that might prevent you from listening to other perspectives?

3. How do you facilitate the concept of "open learner" in your organization? How do you model it?

4. Can you point to examples in history where leaders held on too long to old practices, beliefs, and strategies?

5. What steps can you take to be an open learner?

Wishing you a day of open learning.

"Live as if you were to die tomorrow. Learn as if you were to live forever."
Mahatma Gandhi

REFLECTION #71:
PROTECT THE MISSION

Visionary leaders acknowledge that building an open mind/strong heart culture often requires both pushing and pulling people (and themselves) to places of discomfort. These leaders accept that there may be significant resistance to change, and they must prevent that resistance from disrupting team dynamics. While they embrace their responsibility to create a compelling vision to support their mission, these leaders also know that sometimes impasse is reached, and difficult personnel and strategic decisions must be made. Mindful leaders use creative strategies to avoid ultimatums, but they are too committed to their mission to allow disruptions. They understand that they can't navigate a ship when people are trying to go in different directions and are using different rules to move the vessel. These leaders reluctantly accept that some values and missions simply can't be embraced by some people. They also acknowledge that if you can't "change the people," you often have to "change the people."

1. How do you assess alignment skills of your team members or the organization as a whole?

2. How do you gain alignment in times of significant change?

3. When was the last time you were forced to take action in the face of lack of alignment?

4. How would you describe your skills at leading an unavoidable conflict?

5. Are you so committed to your mission that you are determined not to let naysayers disrupt it? What evidence supports your answer?

Wishing you a mission you are willing to protect.

REFLECTION #72:
DESTROY HIERARCHY

Confident leaders know how to use and trust the strengths of others, and do not rely on bureaucracy and hierarchy for control. These leaders recognize that their most significant impact comes from assembling the right team with a mix of skills, perspectives, experiences, and personalities, and they have no fear associated with others being the best or the brightest of their teams. These confident people do not allow their own egos to block the genius of the organization, and they enthusiastically promote the brilliance of their team members. They understand that the effectiveness of the seniority model of leadership has long expired, and they celebrate their own ability to be the captain without the need to sit on the highest chair. Leaders search for indicators of hierarchy or silo blocks, and they enthusiastically destroy them. These mindful leaders hold people accountable for not building or adhering strictly to hierarchy. They know that true power comes from being at the center of the organization and not on top of it.

1. How do you consciously assemble a team with a variety of experiences and talents that complement and complete your own?

2. How do you honestly feel when team members know more than you do?

3. Where and when have you relied on the strength of others? How are you doing it now?

4. How do you stay conscious of the temptation of ego, and prevent the impact it can have on your leadership?

5. How are you helping the organization let go of the concept of "seniority rules?"

May you exercise your power "with" and not "over."

"...as we let our own light shine, we unconsciously give other people permission to do the same." Marianne Williamson

Mindful leaders know it is important to seek counsel and mentorship while maintaining stable self-confidence and strong, independent decision-making. These thoughtful leaders understand that their relevance and growth depend on being able to see the world through the eyes of others, and they seek mentorship from varied and unlikely people. They create their own personal "board of directors." They ask for ideas and opinions on a variety of topics. When they seek advice, they actually listen and reflect on the advice given. They enjoy brainstorming and testing their conclusions. These leaders are excited about their own continued growth and evolution, and they view the counsel of others as an important conduit to leadership evolution.

1. Who do you go to for mentorship and for testing your conclusions?

2. How often do you seek advice? Are you comfortable asking for help?

3. How do you navigate between seeking input and making your own decision?

4. How do you value diversity in your own personal "board of directors?" Do you have a group like this available to you?

5. How passionate are you about your own growth through others? What practices support this passion?

Wishing you a day filled with good counsel and the freedom to seek it.

"Walk with those seeking truth. Run from those who think they've found it." Deepak Chopra

_____

_____

_____

_____

_____

_____

_____

_____

_____

_____

_____

_____

_____

_____

REFLECTION #74:
ELIMINATE WASTE

Breakthrough leaders acknowledge that they have a significant influence over how employees spend organizational time and resources. These leaders know that they don't have the right to waste company resources and employees' time on meaningless tasks and continuously mundane work. These leaders are thoughtful with their policies, procedures, and assignments, and they acknowledge that when you waste an employee's time, you are essentially wasting a part of their lives. To support the elimination of waste, mindful leaders are passionate about eliminating bureaucracy, often take a record on how employees spend their day, and work as a partner to maximize employee involvement in the right projects. These leaders know that broken relationships and separation can generate waste in the organization, and they work to build unity and a strong organizational community that supports efficiency and fast action. These leaders are keenly aware that time spent at work account for most of our waking hours, and are determined to make those hours matter. They abhor waste of time and resources.

1. Are you conscious of how you contribute or eliminate waste in the lives of those you lead?

2. Do you pay attention to how your team members spend their days at work?

3. What waste or bureaucracy have you eliminated this year?

4. Where do you see opportunities right now to eliminate meaningless work or ineffective policies and procedures?

5. Are you a partner at bringing meaning and significance to most of the work effort?

Wishing you only hours that matter.

REFLECTION #75:
LOVE AND LEADERSHIP

Transformational leaders know that new principles of leadership are required to identify what is appropriate, and to redefine power and the exercise of it. These leaders have educated themselves on the evolution of leadership qualities present during the past half century, and continue to adjust and grow to meet new organizational demands. These leaders are aware of the motivations of the new generations of employees and what they are demanding. They are comfortable with a leadership that could be characterized as "higher ground leadership." Effective leaders are not tied to the leadership language of the past but are constantly seeking, redefining, and articulating their message appropriately for the present culture and moment. In 1995, Dr. Lance Secretan, a leadership consultant before his time, coined the phrase "higher ground leadership" and identified the CASTLE® principles that support it.

C-Courage
A-Authenticity
S-Service
T-Truthfulness
L-Love
E-Effectiveness

In a similar spirit, we offer the THINKLOVE model for your use and reflection. Regardless of what expanded model you choose, without some renewed leadership language that includes principles like THINKLOVE or CASTLE®, many employees will not be truly inspired, nor will they fully embrace the organization or its priorities. Whether the use of the word love is utilized or not, leadership should show evidence of deep caring for those they lead.

"Wherever you find a culture where results are humming, values are working, and people are energized, you will find love at work." Brady Wilson

1. How do you see love playing a role in your leadership?

2. What is your own unique language of leadership? What words of care and concern are prevalent in your leadership discussions?

3. How do you test what language and behavior works for different members of your team? How do you vary your approach?

4. Has your leadership deepened over time? Do you incorporate principles of "higher ground" leadership in it now?

5. Acknowledging that the word love often has a limited connotation, how can we still use its power in organizations?

Wishing you a day standing on higher ground.

REFLECTION #76:
SHOW HUMILITY

Rick Warren said, "True humility isn't thinking less of yourself, it is thinking of yourself less." While that may be a catchy phrase, research shows that it is an accurate characterization of humility. In addition, research shows that humility results in greater effectiveness. A well-written article in the Washington Post by Ashley Merryiman detailed the research on this topic, stating, "Leaders are more powerful when they are humble." She defined humility as, "True humility, scientists have learned, is when someone has an accurate assessment of both his strengths and weaknesses, and he sees all this in the context of the larger whole. He's a part of something far greater than himself. He knows he isn't the center of the universe. And he's both grounded and liberated by this knowledge. Recognizing his abilities, he asks how he can contribute. Recognizing his flaws, he asks how he can grow."

In July 2016's *Personality and Individual Differences*, Duke University researchers reported on a study conducted with 155 participants. At the experiment's onset, some people conceded their opinions weren't always right, and with new evidence they'd change their views. The researchers considered them as intellectually humble. Others were intellectually arrogant; they insisted they were rarely wrong, and they never changed their mind. The intellectual humble participants always performed better at the end of the experiment. And the benefits don't stop there. Studies have shown that those low in humility overreact during conflicts. They strike out when angered and plot their revenge. If they're the actual wrongdoers, they refuse to apologize or accept responsibility. Instead, they blame their victims.

Leading with humility doesn't mean these leaders don't drive performance. Humility is often combined, however, with a trait that Lencioni calls "hunger." This combination propels these leaders to drive their missions with passion and conviction, and with a sense of humility and grace. While they are known to facilitate significant transformations and impact many lives, they always identify with the call to service and never clamor for glory or status. These humble men and women are not driven by their own narcissism, they are propelled by the mission and their people.

1. How do you define humility? Would your team describe you as leading with humility?

2. Were you taught that humility is a great trait for a leader to possess? Did you learn that it was a strength? How might that impact your subconscious willingness to pursue it?

3. Can you admit out loud that you don't have all the answers and still stand in your power? Can you feel proud of your humility?

4. How do you maintain your humility in the face of success? How do you guard against taking too much credit?

Honoring your expression of powerful humility.

_____

_____

_____

_____

_____

_____

_____

_____

_____

_____

_____

_____

REFLECTION #77:
IGNITING SELF-MOTIVATION

Mindful leaders understand that success in motivating their teams to aim higher and perform beyond expectations is only achieved through employee actions. Leaders use their skills of inspiring and motivating to unleash self-motivation throughout the organization. To do this effectively, they spend a great deal of time understanding the diverse values, needs, and motivational factors of those they lead. They work purposefully to align those needs to business goals and objectives.

In the journal "Trends in Cognitive Sciences" (Hughes, 2015), it was noted that self-motivation is not a static feature of our personality nor the outcome of a neurological calculus, but a skill that can be learned and honed. It was further claimed that self-motivation is closely tied to whether we believe we are "in control and making our own decisions" and whether those decisions are endowed with larger meaning.

Transformational leaders know that employee empowerment facilitates self-motivation, and they develop ways to grant employees more control over their daily priorities, schedules, and creative ways of getting work done. Accordingly, these leaders ensure that employees feel they have a meaningful and challenging job and are making a significant contribution to the organization.

1. How are you studying the art of motivating your employees?

2. How do you note and access the level of self-motivation of your team?

3. How do you distribute your personal and organizational power to your team members?

4. What is your own unique way of endowing actions with significance?

5. How are you with pulling your team and being carried by them?

Wishing you a self-motivated day of success.

_____

_____

_____

_____

_____

_____

_____

_____

_____

_____

_____

"The major challenge of most executives is not understanding the practice
of leadership - it is practicing their understanding of leadership."
Marshall Goldsmith

REFLECTION #78:
PSYCHOLOGICAL SAFETY

The "People Analytics" team at Google tackled several human questions from a data perspective, encompassing everything from productivity, boss effectiveness, intellectual challenge appropriateness, team dynamics, and a hundred other variables. In one of their projects, they studied team effectiveness for two years before they determined the consistent factors that made teams productive and impactful. Initially it was hard to pinpoint consistent factors, as many of the great teams were diverse in make-up and norms. The conclusion? The two factors that propelled the teams from good to great was "psychological safety" and "equal voice opportunity" (EVO).

Simon Sinek explored the role of "psychological safety" (the ability to feel safe enough around each other to present ideas, admit failures, take risks, say "I don't know," admit they disagree) in his book *Leaders Eat Last*. He emphasized that effective leaders create psychological safety and understand that without it, everything stays in status quo. Similarly, if some of the team members are more authorized to voice their opinions, psychological safety and EVO are threatened and progress stalls. Effective leaders eliminate barriers to psychological safety and articulate it as a corporate value. They continually look for ways to build foundations of trust and they invite more members to join the organizational circle of trust.

1. How are you building psychological safety in your group right now?

2. Have you had a discussion with your team about designing a circle of trust? How do you guard it?

3. Who can you point to that you as a leader have helped transition from silent to participatory?

4. What is the opportunity for improvement in your leadership style to build greater psychological safety?

5. How can your gatherings be changed to improve both
    psychological safety and EVO?

Wishing you a larger circle of trust.

_____

_____

_____

_____

_____

_____

_____

_____

_____

_____

_____

"When there is no circle of safety we force our employees to expend
their energy to protect themselves from each other."
Simon Sinek

REFLECTION #79:
DIRECTING ORGANIZATIONAL FOCUS

In this world of continuous and overwhelming information, effective leaders understand that directing organizational focus is the key to achieving breakthrough results. These leaders understand that to become genuinely productive, it is necessary to direct attention and build mental models of what the team needs to focus on, on a day-to-day basis. These mindful leaders reinforce organizational direction by creating a culture that consciously chooses priorities and embraces the authority to say no. They communicate these priorities repeatedly and align them to the company's overall vison and mission. They acknowledge that there may be distractions and interruptions that will arise from a crisis that needs immediate attention, but they quickly refocus their teams on the goal at hand. They are steadfast in their decision-making by refusing to overreact to every crisis and change priorities based on the flavor of the day. These leaders navigate their teams to ensure they stay focused on the true priorities.

1. How do your conversations drive the focus of your teams?

2. How do you help your teams to eliminate distraction and noises?

3. How are you visually highlighting what is important right now?

4. How do you manage multiple priorities and unexpected crises with clarity and focus?

5. How do you bring clarity and transparency to the decision-making process to establish priorities?

Wishing you a day focused on doing the right things.

"Beware lest you lose the substance by grasping at the shadow."

Aesop

_____

_____

_____

_____

_____

_____

_____

_____

_____

_____

_____

_____

_____

_____

_____

Breakthrough leaders understand that SMART (specific, measurable, achievable, relevant, time-bound) goals alone won't produce transformational results. In fact, the very definition which includes "achievable" could limit thinking and performance. Instead, these leaders push for a combination of SMART goals coupled with breakthrough targets. These leaders know that these stretch targets have been proven to shift attention to possible new futures and have sparked new energy in companies such as GE and Toyota, who live by them. Breakthrough leaders have the ability to move BHAGs (big, hairy, audacious goals, coined by Jim Collins and Jerry I. Porras in *Built to Last*) into sub-goals, identify specific actions for targeting them, and to align the organization around achieving the ultimate result. These leaders ensure that they create a feeling of palpable team spirit and that the employees own both the goal and the results, so BHAGs are not only tangible but energizing and focused. Inspirational leaders know that to deliver sustainable transformation through goal setting, the process must incite enthusiasm, gain buy-in, ensure focus, and show measurable achievement.

1. What BHAGs are you and your organization pursuing now?

2. What are important SMART goals that support the BHAG?

3. How did you produce ownership for the goal?

4. How do you hold each other accountable for achieving the stated goals/objectives?

5. How have you helped embed the truth that your organization can see beyond SMART goals to what is possible? What breakthrough are you most proud of that you and your team accomplished together?

Wishing you a day of audacious goal achievement.

REFLECTION #81:
TALK THE WALK

It is widely accepted that leaders must "walk the talk" to lead authentic transformation, but less attention has been paid to how remarkable leaders "talk the walk." Bill Taylor, cofounding editor of *Fast Company* magazine and author, writes in *Harvard Business Review*, "To talk the walk is to be able to explain, in language that is compelling to colleagues and customers, why what they do matters." He emphasizes that it is a critical skill for leaders to build, and is a real and strong competitive advantage. He adds that, "The only sustainable form of business leadership is through leadership," and "Leaders that think differently about their business invariably talk about it differently, as well" (Taylor, 2014). He concludes the article by declaring, "Behind it all, at the heart of the company's approach to strategy, service, and culture, is a language system that defines life inside the organization and reminds everyone what really drives it."

Mindful leaders have helped to create their own company "language system" and speak about it with clarity and passion every day. They are committed to knowing how to talk the walk, and they practice this skill continuously.

1. As you think about your own leadership and the language you use every day, what are some of the common themes?

2. Are you intentional and purposeful in the words you use, or do you pretty much just say what comes to mind?

3. How can you improve this skill, and what impact would it have on your power to drive employee engagement?

4. What implications does a "talking the walk" objective have for on-boarding? Communications? Goal setting?

5. How can you create a healthy and effective organizational language system?

Wishing you a day of powerful, purposeful talk.

_____

_____

_____

_____

_____

_____

_____

_____

_____

_____

_____

"Leadership is about making others better as a result of your presence and making sure that impact lasts in your absence." Sheryl Sandberg

REFLECTION #82:
MANAGING ORGANIZATIONAL RISK

Transformational leaders know that managing the risk of employee disengagement is just as important as managing any technical or security risk. According to studies by Gallup and the Queens School of Business, in the U.S. alone, it is estimated that in 2017 unengaged employees cost U.S. organizations about $605 billion. The studies highlight that organizations with employees who say they are engaged enjoy considerably higher productivity and profitability ratings, combined with less turnover and absenteeism. Organizations with low employee engagement scores experienced 18 percent lower productivity, 16 percent lower profitability, 37 percent lower job growth, and 65 percent lower share prices over time. Accordingly, leaders who deliver organizational success have strategies and plans on the organizational level to engage employees, but they also embed the goal of engagement in their daily leadership responsibilities. They measure employee engagement, finding reliable ways to actively gauge how engaged their employees are. These mindful leaders know that they play a significant role in that engagement, and they interact with their employees in a way that improves that engagement. They communicate frequently, insist on fairness, and for work to be transparent. Whether introverts or extroverts, these leaders are "felt," throughout the organization and the organization's results are improved because of it.

1. How would you rate the engagement of your team members? Engagement of the organization as a whole?

2. What impact have you had on the engagement level?

3. What strategies are you using to increase engagement throughout the organization?

4. Where do you see signs of the effects of disengagement?

5. How is the organization valuing the creation of employee engagement, and how are they holding leaders accountable for managing the risk of employee disengagement?

Wishing you a day of active engagement.

_____

_____

_____

_____

_____

_____

_____

_____

_____

_____

_____

_____

_____

_____

_____

_____

_____

_____

_____

_____

_____

_____

REFLECTION #83: SELF-KNOWLEDGE

Conscious leaders understand that the first step in doing power differently is always about self-examination—a deep inquiry designed to help them understand their own beliefs, behaviors, blind spots, prejudices, and what is driving them. These leaders know that this inward journey is a necessary part of leadership. Just as a mirror provides the information required to adjust physical appearance, introspection provides the information needed to adjust the behavior of a conscious leader. Rather than resist the work needed to promote personal awareness and growth, they dedicate time and commit resources in acknowledgement of their leadership responsibilities.

As Warren Bennis stated in *On Becoming a Leader*, "No true and remarkable leader sets out to be a leader. People set out to live their lives, expressing themselves fully. So, the initial point is not to become a leader. The point is to become yourself, to use yourself completely—all your skills, gifts, and energies—to make your vision manifest. You must withhold nothing. You must, in sum, become the person you started out to be, and enjoy the process of becoming" (Bennis, 1989).

Conscious leaders embody this concept and build this self-examination practice into their daily workflow, and use it as they would any other important data. They never stop discovering who they really are.

1. What practice do you use for self-examination? What information is it providing you?

2. How are you expressing yourself fully? What has been the impact of that expression?

3. What vision are you helping to manifest? How are your unique gifts at work in that manifestation?

4. Does the idea of "becoming" make sense to you? Are you enjoying the process?

5. During these reflections, what are some of the insights you have gained about yourself?

Wishing you a day of becoming fully and completely you.

_____

_____

_____

_____

_____

_____

_____

_____

_____

_____

"Who looks outside, dreams; who looks inside, awakes."
Carl Jung

REFLECTION #84:
PROMOTING SELF-MANAGEMENT

"In a few hundred years, when the history of our time will be written from a long-term perspective, it is likely that the most important event historians will see is not technology, not the Internet, not e-commerce. It is an unprecedented change in the human condition. For the first time—literally—substantial and rapidly growing numbers of people have choices. For the first time, they will have to manage themselves. And society is totally unprepared for it" (Peter Drucker, *Managing Oneself*, 2000).

Two decades later, it is hard to argue with this quote, especially with a mobile and remote workforce, extensive globalization, and complex technology. For centuries, workers have done what they were told to do and were "managed" by others. Today's complex world makes it difficult to visually follow our team members even with deep and vast KPIs (Key Performance Indicators), balanced scorecards, etc., which tend to show performance after it has happened. The real challenge now is to facilitate "self-management" and allow the leaders to hire the right people who can lead themselves to extraordinary results.

Exceptional leaders understand that self-management and motivation are the ultimate goals of their leadership, and they build systems to allow their team members to self-manage. These systems include real-time data and the ability, authority, and freedom to adjust in response to this data, coupled with rewards and recognition for such ownership. The leaders who are passionate about creating this environment are transforming the idea of management and are expanding free thought throughout the organization. These exceptional leaders are creating organizations that are prepared for tomorrow.

1. How are you embedding the concept of self-management into your organization?

2. What changes have you made in your leadership style to promote it?

3. What are the roadblocks in your organization for self-management? What beliefs are these roadblocks based on?

4. What are the possibilities for new thinking around the concept of self-management?

5. How is your leadership needed to promote it?

Honoring your ability to let others self-manage.

REFLECTION #85:
LEAD WITH INTENTION

In her book *Leading with Intention: Every Moment Is a Choice*, Mindy Hall, Ph.D., concludes that leaders who lead with intention deliver superior operational and financial performance. She further emphasizes that every interaction—whether presenting to an entire organization or talking one-on-one with a colleague—is an opportunity to influence and inspire others to achieve extraordinary results. She states, "Your ability to do that depends on two factors: How aware you are of your impact, and, the care and discipline with which you choose your actions, day by day, moment by moment" (Hall, 2014).

In other words, how intentional you are.

Leading with intention makes the connection between leadership behavior and the bottom line, and it challenges leaders to make a profound, deliberate mark on both the organization they lead and the world around them. The ideas include:

- Every leadership interaction is an opportunity
- Every leadership action has an impact
- Every leadership moment is a choice

Effective leaders set daily intentions and build their workday around those intentions. They choose wisely how they spend their time and energy, acknowledging their significant impact.

1. What intention have you set for today? For the week?

2. How do you determine if you have met that intention?

3. Do you document or clarify your intention in any way?

4. How do you make that intention visible?

5. What opportunities have you manifested from your intention setting?

Wishing you a day filled with clear intentions and positive impact.

_____

_____

_____

_____

_____

_____

_____

"When the whole world is silent, even one voice becomes powerful."
Malala Yousafzai

Transformational leaders often know that other leaders of the world—near and far, past and present—provide many lessons in leadership. These leaders are constantly reading, attending seminars, and researching the leadership profession, and they understand that the best teaching is often found from talking to and watching other leaders. Transformational leaders often know which leaders resonate with them, and they often are drawn to one or two specifically.

While religious reference may not be the norm, the document of leadership of Jesus is often studied. As noted in *Forbes Magazine* recently, "You don't have to be Christian to learn leadership lessons from Jesus. Despite being executed as a criminal, Jesus managed to start a faith that now has more than two billion followers and has lasted almost two thousand years. Clearly, Jesus knew a thing or two about leadership" (Loftus, 2014).

Ten characteristics of His leadership have been described as:

1. Jesus was willing to invest in people others would have dismissed. Consider the disciples. They were not the religious elite, yet Jesus used them to start the church.

2. Jesus shared his power, responsibility, and ownership. Consider how Jesus sent the disciples out on their own to do the work. No micromanagement.

3. Jesus was focused on his succession plan. He consistently reminded the disciples he wouldn't always be with them. Of course, he was still the "leader," but he was always looking for ways for his work to survive without him. He very deliberately prepared the disciples to take over the ministry. He pushed people beyond what they felt capable of doing.

4. Jesus practiced servant leadership better than anyone. He constantly reminded his team that leadership was responsibility, not status. He washed feet—he didn't ask for his feet to be washed.

5. Jesus was laser-like in his vision. Regardless of the persecutions or distractions, he kept focused on what he was here to achieve.

6. Jesus sought guidance and feedback. Jesus constantly slipped away to spend time with God.

7. Jesus motivated and inspired. Jesus knew what motivated transformation in his people. Matthew was a tax collector who wanted to exchange that lifestyle for one with more meaning and purpose. Jesus was not afraid to make huge requests of people. "Follow me" meant the disciples had to drop their agendas to do so.

8. Jesus cared more about people than about rules and regulations. Jesus was a notorious rule-breaker. He was willing to jeopardize himself personally by breaking the rules to help someone in need.

9. Jesus told stories and spoke in a language his people could hear and understand. He didn't use corporate speak. He was a master storyteller.

Jesus always stood up for what he believed in and spoke truth to power. From religious to political leaders, he never backed down or backed away.

Certainly, there are other leaders who may resonate more fully with you to be studied and learned from. Your assignment is to choose a few that work for you and conduct the inquiry.

1. What leaders–past or present, real or fictional–have you learned from?

2. Do you have a practice of speaking to other leaders about leadership issues?

3. How are you taking lessons learned by others in the past and the present, and incorporating them into your work today so you don't have to repeat those lessons?

4. What leadership characteristics attributed to Jesus resonate specifically with you? Which ones do you admire?

5. Name the top ten personal characteristics you would want for
   your own leadership.

Wishing you a day filled with the lessons from the world's greatest leaders.

*"The teacher who is indeed wise does not bid you to enter the house of
his wisdom but rather leads you to the threshold of your mind."*
Kahil Gibran

REFLECTION #87:
IGNITE JOY

Memorable leaders believe in and strive to create joy in the workplace. These leaders understand that an atmosphere of fun and happiness supports long-term organizational success and productivity. Consider this story: An excited Kirt Womack of the Thiokol factory in Utah sprinted into his manager's office on the first day of spring and asked if the folks on the factory floor could do something fun—say, head outside and fly paper airplanes—if they met their quota two hours early. The manager wrinkled his brow and vetoed the idea. Kirt persisted, "Well, then, what if we exceed our quota by 50 percent?" Figuring he had nothing to lose, the manager finally gave in. Later that day, at one thirty, the manager checked on things and found that his employees had reached 110 percent of their quota. By 3:00 p.m., they'd surpassed 150 percent. The airplanes were launched, laughter rang out, and the energy of the team was visibly lifted.

Studies have shown that happiness actually has economic value and it can play an important role in changing behavior and transforming companies. Remarkable leaders know that there is a direct link between the moods, behavior, and actions of people, and these leaders view "fun at work" as a platform for employees to go the extra mile. These leaders not only look for ways to inject joy in the workplace, they bring a personal sense of joy to their leadership and the work of their organization. They take their work seriously—but never themselves.

1. How do you bring a sense of playfulness to work?

2. Do you ever hear laughter in the halls?

3. Would your employees describe your organization as a fun place to work?

4. What are some of the joyful things your employees do?

5. Is there a sense of joy around the organization's purpose?

Wishing you a day filled with joy and laughter.

_____

_____

_____

_____

_____

_____

_____

_____

_____

_____

_____

_____

_____

_____

_____

_____

_____

_____

_____

_____

_____

_____

REFLECTION #88:
COLLECTIVE LEADERSHIP

One of four future leadership trends that have been identified by the Center for Creative Leadership is "collective leadership." Instead of looking at only the individual's capacity as a leader, as the world becomes more complex, organizations will depend more on the capability of leadership throughout the organization. "There is a transition occurring from the old paradigm in which leadership resided in a person or role, to a new one in which leadership is a collective process that is spread throughout networks of people. The question will change from, 'Who are the leaders?' to 'What conditions do we need for leadership to flourish in the network? How do we spread leadership capacity throughout the organization and democratize leadership?'" (Cullen, et al., 2012).

Many leaders have already embraced the concept of collective leadership, and their commitment to distributing power is felt by their teams. These leaders know that leadership doesn't only reside in individuals, it exists in the culture of their organizations. These leaders are known not solely for their individual feats but by the spirit and effectiveness of their teams and organizations.

1. How are you building systems and processes to embed collective leadership?

2. How would your teams describe the state of power distribution?

3. How would the world describe this distribution within your team?

4. How can you improve your culture of leadership?

5. What current conditions are barriers to this culture?

Wishing you a day surrounded by many leaders.

"I alone cannot change the world, but I can cast a stone across the waters to create many ripples." Mother Teresa

REFLECTION #89:
DEFINING TRANSFORMATIONAL LEADERSHIP

In *Psychology Today*, writer Ronald Riggio identified four components of transformational leadership, which are sometimes referred to as the four I's:

1. Idealized Influence (II)—the transformational leader serves as an ideal role model for followers; the leader walks the talk and is admired for this.
2. Inspirational Motivation (IM)—the transformational leader has the ability to inspire and motivate followers. Combined, these first two I's are what constitute the transformational leader's charisma.
3. Individualized Consideration (IC)—the transformational leader demonstrates genuine concern for the needs and feelings of followers. This personal attention to each follower is a key element in bringing out their very best efforts.
4. Intellectual Stimulation (IS)—the transformational leader challenges followers to be innovative and creative. A common misunderstanding is that transformational leaders are "soft," but the truth is they constantly challenge followers to higher levels of performance.

Riggio further stated, "Research evidence clearly shows that groups led by transformational leaders have higher levels of performance and satisfaction than groups led by other types of leaders. Why? Because transformational leaders hold positive expectations for followers, believing that they can and will do their best. As a result, they inspire, empower, and stimulate followers to exceed normal levels of performance. And transformational leaders focus on and care about followers and their personal needs and development" (Riggio, 2014).

Transformational leaders answer the following questions in the affirmative. How do you answer them? Where are you strong in your answers? Where are your opportunities for growth?

1. I would never require a follower to do something I wouldn't do myself.

2. My followers would say they know what I stand for.

3. Inspiring others has always come easy to me.

4. My followers have told me that my enthusiasm and positive energy are infectious.

5. My followers would say I am very attentive to their needs and concerns.

6. Even though I could easily do a task myself, I delegate it to expand my followers' skills.

7. Team creativity and innovation are the keys to success.

8. I encourage my followers to question their most basic way of thinking.

Here's to your journey as a transformational leader.

_____

_____

_____

_____

_____

_____

_____

REFLECTION # 90:
COURAGEOUS CONVERSATIONS

Breakthrough leaders understand the importance of, and are skilled in, the art of courageous conversation. They have a deep commitment to navigating sensitive interactions with their teams. They also understand that difficult things simply must be said, and they consider these language interactions as central to their leadership. These leaders approach courageous conversations with the intent to build trust, strengthen relationships, and improve performance. They plan for these significant moments, and they help other leaders of the organization develop skills to have these interactions, as well. These leaders are committed to speaking their truth even when it isn't easy, knowing that leaving important issues unaddressed stalls progress and impedes transformation efforts. As Susan Scott, author of *Fierce Conversations*, said, "While no one conversation is guaranteed to change the trajectory of your company or life, any single conversation can. Like it or not, you build influence and 'make your luck' one conversation at a time. The conversations that take the most courage—those in which you speak candidly and listen openly—are those which make the biggest impact. They are what I call courageous conversations, and they create a pathway to building the relationships, influence, and outcomes you want in every area of your life" (Scott, 2002). Mindful leaders know that courageous conversations are a gift to the organization, and they manage and lead those conversations with intention and commitment.

1. How comfortable are you with candid conversations when you are delivering "bad" news?

2. Are there conversations that you are avoiding right now? What is dying to be said?

3. Are there words stuck inside you that would make a difference in your ability to lead?

4. What support do you need to be bolder in your conversations?

5. What is the most courageous conversation you have had in your life? What difference did it make?

Wishing you a day filled with bold, meaningful conversations.

"Be brave enough to start a conversation that matters."
Margaret Wheatley

Effective leaders know that when workplace optimism is present, employees are attracted to possibility rather than idolizing problems. This belief in possibility drives workplace curiosity—an attitude of wonder about the company's challenges and how to solve its problems. These leaders know that their personal level of optimism has an impact on whether or not the culture is optimistic. They accept that they have a broader responsibility because of this influence, and they intentionally work to create a "positive outlook" environment within the organization as a whole. *Inc. Magazine* identified ten leadership characteristics that leaders embodied to build a culture of optimism (Murphy, 2016). Review the 10 characteristics and make a note of how you embody them.

- They knew their employees' strengths, and focused on aligning employee strengths and their work.
- They got to know the whole employee; they knew what their employees' passions, hobbies, and goals were outside of work.
- They let employees "in" on things. They ensured employees were aware of, and could give input on topics important to them, their livelihood, motivation, and future.
- They checked the "pulse" of the office daily; they didn't wait for the annual survey to understand the vibe of their company.
- Their organizational and personal purpose were aligned. It's been shown that less than 20 percent of leaders know their personal purpose.
- They offered flexible work arrangements. Four out of five employees say work flexibility is important when considering a new job. Yet, fewer than one in five have work flexibility.
- They hold regular one-on-ones. They schedule them and don't leave them to chance.
- They set both team and individual goals. Teams are accountable to one another.
- They offer varying work experiences.
- They make sure the organizational values are real, articulated, and enforced.

1. What's the current state of your organization's optimism?

2. What role are you playing in the creation of it?

3. What evidence can you show that would support a belief in "it's all good?"

4. Of the ten behaviors above, which ones are you incorporating?

5. Where are your areas of opportunity for being a leader who can create and recreate a culture of optimism?

Wishing you the power to help create a culture of optimism.

_____

_____

_____

_____

_____

_____

_____

_____

_____

_____

_____

_____

_____

_____

Courageous leaders understand that authentic leadership demands the expression of the authentic self. As *Harvard Business Review* says, "If you try to lead like someone else—say, Jack Welch, Richard Branson, or Michael Dell—you will fail. Employees will not follow a CEO who invests little of himself in his leadership behaviors" (Goffee & Jones, 2005). Quite simply, people want to be led by someone "real." HBR continues, "This is partly a reaction to the turbulent times we live in. It is also a response to the public's widespread disenchantment with politicians and businesspeople. We all suspect that we're being duped."

Mindful leadership demands the expression of an authentic self. Today more than ever, organizations are growing dissatisfied with sleek, airbrushed leadership, and they long to see leaders be themselves, so they, in turn, can show up authentically.

HBR goes on to say, "But while the expression of an authentic self is necessary for great leadership, the concept of authenticity is often misunderstood, not least by leaders themselves. They often assume that authenticity is an innate quality—that a person is either authentic or not. In fact, authenticity is a quality that others must attribute to you. No leader can look into a mirror and say, 'I am authentic.' A person cannot be authentic on his or her own. Authenticity is largely defined by what other people see in you and, as such, can to a great extent be controlled by you. If authenticity were purely an innate quality, there would be little you could do to manage it and, therefore, little you could do to make yourself more effective" (Goffee & Jones, 2005).

Mindful leaders have an intention to show up authentically, and they are constantly on a search for what that means for them. They work on it. Their teams feel their intent and they move in synchronicity with commitment for authenticity. Based on this collective approach, the organization develops a culture of authenticity.

1. Would your teams define you as authentic?

2. How is that answer impacting your culture?

3. What practices in your life are allowing you to be more authentic?

4. What fears or obstacles get in the way of you being your authentic self?

5. How are you building a culture of authenticity?

Wishing you a day of creating a culture that's real for you and others.

_____

_____

_____

_____

_____

"Be yourself, because the people who mind don't matter and
the people who matter don't mind." Dr. Seuss

Trusted leaders acknowledge they have endured and surpassed some sort of failure. In fact, they acknowledge that many of their most rewarding opportunities and lessons were fueled by some painful or challenging experience. These experiences could include a bad hire, an ineffective decision, a poor investment—or a myriad of things, large and small, that just didn't work out in the manner desired or expected. *Forbes'* writers have described failure as "the most powerful source for know-how and understanding. It teaches you about survival, renewal, and reinvention of yourself and the organization you are leading" (Llopis, 2012).

The challenge for leaders is to be able to "sit with" the failure fully and take its lessons. Mindful leaders do that—they never run from failure or deny it. In fact, they often wear the survival and transcendence of it like a badge of honor. These leaders understand that they can determine someone's character by simply asking: "What were your three greatest failures and how did you overcome them?" If the respondent can't think of three, they either haven't stretched themselves enough (they may be extremely risk adverse) or they are not valuing the benefits of failure (and thus are too proud to examine—or even admit—their failures). True leaders don't hide from the past, they incorporate the consequential lessons learned. They treat failure as a positive sign they didn't live squarely inside their comfort zones.

1. What were your three greatest failures, and how did you overcome them?

2. How do you stand firmly in your leadership and still admit errors?

3. How do you live and deal with the failures of your team members?

4. How do you distinguish between incompetence and appropriate failure?

5. How do you maintain your self-confidence in the face of failure?

Here's to remembering all the times you fell—
and how powerfully you got back up.

_____

_____

_____

_____

_____

_____

_____

_____

_____

_____

_____

_____

_____

_____

_____

_____

_____

_____

_____

_____

_____

REFLECTION #94:
CREATING A "CHECK ME" CULTURE

Conscious leaders know that the organization's transformation and evolution depend on the ability of its members to authentically agree to a "check me" culture. In this environment, leaders openly acknowledge they have blind spots and intentionally ask their team members for help. These leaders model the courage and commitment needed to ask others to "stand in their commitments" with them because they know that true change is difficult to accomplish alone. Following the leader's example, strong organizations have team members who constantly check one another's work and consistently hold each other accountable. They agree that execution excellence depends on a "check me" culture, and teams are excited about helping each other find out what went wrong and why commitments weren't met. There is a positive energy around this exploration and a focus on the mission of the organization. These organizations know that they can only aim higher and dream bigger if everyone has a standing invitation to "collectively correct."

1. How do you respond when someone points out that you didn't fulfill a commitment, perhaps as simple as answering an email?

2. How do you feel when a misstep is pointed out?

3. What invitation have you extended for others to "stand in your commitments" with you?

4. How can you improve your pursuit of execution excellence with a "check me" culture right now?

5. How can we inject more excitement and passion around creating a "check me" culture?

Wishing you the courage to promote a "check me" culture.

"Mistakes only cost you when you don't acknowledge them."
Russel Simmons

REFLECTION #95:
YOUR LEADERSHIP INVESTMENT

Impactful leaders understand that redefining power in the world depends on their own personal unfolding. They know why they want to be a leader, and they invest time and resources into their personal leadership development. They do not rely solely on corporate-sponsored programs but are eager to invest in their own growth. These mindful leaders dedicate space every day to the study of and reflection on leadership in general, and their performance as a leader in particular. These leaders know that regardless of their deep technical expertise or advanced intellect, the greatest impact they can have is in how they lead. They also know the leadership journey is never truly over and they set goals for a greater leadership capacity. These mindful leaders know that they should grow and evolve year after year, demonstrating ever-greater depth in their leadership commitment.

1. When was the last time you attended a class or other formal activity to further your leadership?

2. What is your leadership improvement practice outside of your company's programs?

3. How much time do you spend on your leadership pursuit or reflection daily?

4. What leadership investment commitments do you employ that those you lead could readily identify?

5. What return have you and others seen on your leadership investment?

May your leadership ROI exceed expectations.

"One can choose to go back toward safety or forward toward growth. Growth must be chosen again and again; fear must be overcome again and again."

Abraham Maslow

REFLECTION #96:
HONORING OTHER VIEWPOINTS

Transformational leaders have an ability to see both sides of the story and resist the urge to hang tightly to their first conclusions. Dr. Phil said, "No matter how flat you make a pancake, it still has two sides." These leaders drive the members of their organizations to have open minds and be open learners, and to create frameworks that test their conclusions from a variety of perspectives.

A study was done in the early '80s that had random volunteers broken into two groups. The first group was asked why they should buy a VCR. The second group was asked why they should not buy a VCR. Afterward, they were asked the opposite question. Both groups struggled to answer the opposing question after they had firmly answered the first. Other studies have found similar results. Simply, after we have reached a conclusion in a certain framework, we find it hard to see the other side of the story. In law school, students are forced to break this attachment by not knowing what side of the case they will argue until they enter the room.

Mindful leaders know that "attached thinking" destroys creativity and innovation. These leaders are always looking for new ways to think about important topics, and they listen to friend and foe alike. They stand on the lookout for frameworks that limit the organization's thinking, and they reward people who can view a problem from different angles. These leaders facilitate "thinking freedom." Through their respect of different viewpoints, they expand the opportunity for organizational unity. No team member is ostracized because of a different viewpoint.

1. How would you rate your ability to see opposing viewpoints?

2. Do you have a tendency to think the other viewpoint is intellectually flawed? What deep-rooted beliefs do you have that may get in the way of thinking freedom?

3. Can you point to a time when you have changed your mind on a significant conclusion?

4. How are you helping to build an organization that tests beliefs and perspectives?

5. What role does diversity play in the pursuit of thinking freedom?

Wishing you a day of fresh perspectives and new ideas.

REFLECTION #97:
PEACE WITHIN

Conscious leaders understand that one of their greatest leadership strengths comes from peace with and within self. These leaders know that until they find an inner calm and self-acceptance, they cannot facilitate these productive traits in others. They accept that in turbulent, changing, uncertain times, an organization's ability to thrive depends on the employees' ability to develop an inner narrative that supports inner peace regardless of outward circumstances. These leaders understand, however, that inner peace, like passion, is displayed differently for every human being—there is no one outward face of peace within. For instance, some leaders are very peaceful loudly while some are very peaceful quietly. Both personalities can combine peace with passion and use both internal states working together to produce organizational momentum.

Mindful leaders go beyond the old formula of action that concludes that effort and activity alone produce results. Instead, these leaders know their internal state informs their external actions, and that these external actions determine the nature and quality of their interactions and relationships with those around them. They also accept that simply standing still may often be the appropriate action. Ultimately, they use a practice of inner peace and stillness to access their inner wisdom and gain greater clarity for right action.

1. How do you pay attention to your own internal state before you start your day?

2. When have you recognized your internal state influencing the quality of your external actions? How did those actions determine your interactions with those around you and the results you collectively created?

3. How do you feel about the words "peace within?" Do they sound passive or powerful?

4. What practice in your life supports you in "returning to peace" when you find yourself in a state that doesn't serve you or your organization?

5. What belief system supports your inner peace? Hope? Optimism? Faith?

Wishing you a day filled with internal and external peace.

_____

_____

_____

_____

_____

_____

_____

"You find peace not by rearranging the circumstances of your
life, but by realizing who you are at the deepest level."
Eckhart Tolle

REFLECTION #98:
YOUR LEADERSHIP LEGACY

In *Strengths Based Leadership: A Landmark Study of Great Leaders, Teams, and the Reasons Why We Follow*, author Tom Rath concluded, "Perhaps the ultimate test of a leader is not what they are able to do in the here and now, but instead what continues to grow long after they are gone" (Rath, 2008). This conclusion has been reiterated in a variety of ways by leadership analysts and in leadership commentaries. Just google "leadership legacy" and you will find a variety of thoughts on this topic.

Mindful leaders understand the truth of legacy and they operate with their personal "end" in mind throughout their leadership journey. These leaders understand that while most leaders are never mentioned again when they leave a job or an organization, some leaders are very much remembered. Unfortunately, many of our leaders aren't remembered fondly. However, some leaders have powerful positive legacies that live on for years, continuing to make positive impacts in staff meetings, presentations, and in the lunchroom. We quote them, we follow their examples and we stand on their shoulders.

Visionary leaders are not drawn to legacy to feed their own egos. These leaders are conscious of legacy due to a deep desire to have a positive impact on the world around them, and a humble acceptance that their leadership brand becomes part of the overall brand of the organization. Leaders with a positive legacy achieved it in different ways, but some common themes include:

1. A strong vision for the company and its culture
2. An understanding of the impact leaders have on others, and their ability to teach that truth to others
3. A commitment to improve that impact over time
4. A deep desire to pass on the best of themselves while acknowledging and owning the not-so-perfect parts. These leaders write their legacies every day, and they lead others to "start with the end in mind."

1. How would you describe your desired leadership legacy?

2. What is your own unique "best of self" you want to leave behind?

3. What leaders have left a legacy that you remember?

4. How did those leaders impact your own leadership and desired legacy?

5. How will the people you are honored to lead be different because you were there?

May you always be fondly remembered.

_____

_____

_____

_____

_____

_____

_____

_____

_____

_____

_____

_____

_____

_____

Leaders who lead differently are not confined to the limited corporate objectives of the past, nor do they see a conflict between people, planet, and profit. These leaders know they are called to take care of all three concerns of the organization, and they balance the pursuit of their corporate missions with this triple bottom line in mind. This pursuit is referred to as the "economics of mutuality." Jay Jakub, a president of Mars Corporation, noted: "If you want to make money for a year you ask one set of questions, but if you want to make money for one hundred years you ask different questions. The hundred-year questions revolve around mutuality and sustainability, and challenge the purely profit-driven approach to business rooted in Milton Friedman's economic theory" (Purpose in Leadership, 2014).

Taking profit, planet, and people seriously in the corporate environment means identifying and implementing metrics to measure performance in all three of these bottom-line variables.

Jakub is part of a growing list of corporate leaders who are embedding corporate social responsibility into their daily business instead of isolating it in a foundation. Mindful leaders also understand that their corporate mission must be aligned with their personal leadership values. These leaders model the triple bottom line in how they live their lives. They are known for their concern for a sustainable world, energized people, and healthy profits.

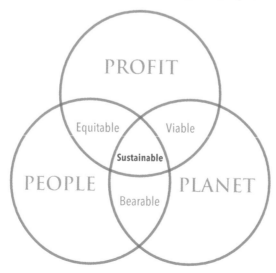

1. How are you as a leader taking care of your people, your planet, and your profit?

2. Are you focused on one over the others?

3. How are you modeling these concerns in your own leadership? Your personal life?

4. What belief system may be driving your focus?

5. How can you expand your approach and make it real to your organization?

Wishing you a day of balancing people, planet, and profit.

REFLECTION #100: THINKLOVE

Leaders who transform their companies and the world can be characterized as simply "doing power differently." These leaders know who they are, what they stand for, and they reflect their true selves in word and action. These mindful leaders inspire trust and seek out ways to break down separation and create unity throughout the organization. They know they are not always right, and they take comfort in that truth, believing fully in the genius that exists within their organizations. When transformational leaders emerge, people rise up and unite in a higher purpose and the world moves in concert with their direction, knowing that the external is manifesting what exists internally. These leaders devote time to self-exploration. Most important, leaders who do power differently spend time day after day touching those they are honored to lead, knowing with certainty that the greatest gift is theirs to receive. They integrate a healthy balance of masculine and feminine energy into the world of work, and they have the courage to speak uncomfortable truths and navigate through storms of resistance. They move in the world with unshakable confidence but understand that each day brings an opportunity for acquired knowledge, learning, and growth.

Great leaders understand there are thousands of ways to listen. They know that transformation often burns and bruises, but in the end, it results in a resilience and strength that is unmatched in places of comfort. Through it all, they demonstrate unbridled optimism and hope. They realize that their honorable position of leadership will demand they have the courage to be vulnerable. They will model this vulnerability in their organization and show that embracing it is neither weak nor damaging. These leaders also manage their energy through attention to physical, emotional, mental, and spiritual health, and they infuse the organization with their enthusiastic spirit. Above all, these leaders accept that this moment demands they personally contribute to the redefinition of power, the eradication of its abuse, and the elimination of injustice. These leaders know that their contribution and commitment will ensure that doing power differently will become the standard of leadership.

Final Question: What is your final declaration for activating your true power?

_____

_____

_____

_____

_____

_____

_____

_____

_____

"Power without love is reckless and abusive, and love
without power is sentimental and anemic."
Martin Luther King Jr.

Final Message

Congratulations on completing one hundred days of activating your true power. Reaching this milestone indicates your firm and serious commitment to be a leader who is willing to release the leadership paradigm of the past and embrace a new, healthier form of leadership. With your leadership practice, you join a multitude of leaders who have declared that the world of work can be a place where we contribute our gifts fully and we feel uplifted in the process. It is clear that all of us have a role in the demanded shift of power's expression, and your commitment moves us one step closer to accomplishing it.

We also hope that the materials provided sparked your own unique thinking about how to balance an open mind and a strong heart at your workplace, and you had the opportunity to discuss these concepts with your teams. As we said throughout the guidebook, THINKLOVE was designed for individual personalization and customization to fit your own circumstances. Likewise, the reflections were created to allow you to pick and choose as appropriate to enhance your own leadership growth. We understand that leadership evolution is a never-ending pursuit, and different circumstances call for different conversations.

We promise that your one hundred days' investment of time and thought will reap returns over and over again, both to you and those you lead. We hope you continue the conversations around a ThinkLove philosophy with us, so together we can make this evolved leadership style the norm.

Finally, it was our great honor to have you with us for this part of the journey. As a member of the movement, you are invited to join us at www.thinkloveleadership.com and www.facebook.com\thinkloveadership.

"Let us all be the leaders we wish we had." Simon Sinek

BIBLIOGRAPHY

Bennis, Warren. *On Becoming a Leader*. Basic Books, 1989. Reflection #83

"Developing Leaders: Today's Methods vs. Tomorrow's Problems." *Center for Creative Leadership*, accessed March 14, 2018. https://www.ccl.org/articles/leading-effectively-articles/developing-leaders-todays-methods-vs-tomorrows-problems-2/. Reflection #88

Drucker, Peter F. *Managing Oneself*. Harvard Business Press, 2008. Reflection #84

Gilbert, Elizabeth. *Big Magic: Creative Living Beyond Fear*. Riverhead Books, 2016. Reflection #32

Goffee, Rob, and Jones, Gareth. "Managing Authenticity: The Paradox of Great Leadership," *Harvard Business Review*, December 200https://hbr. org/2005/12/managing-authenticity-the-paradox-of-great-leadership. Reflection #92

Groysberg, Boris, and Slind, Michael. "Leadership Is a Conversation," *Harvard Business Review*, June 201https://hbr.org/2012/06/leadership-is-a-conversation. Reflection #3

Hall, Mindy. *Leading with Intention: Every Moment Is a Choice*. Copper Bay Press, 201Reflection #85

Hawkins, David R. *Power Vs. Force. The Hidden Determinants of Human Behavior.* Hay House, 2002, page 1.

Lattimer, Christina. "Open Learner". www.peopledevelopmentmagazine.com (2013). Reflection #70

Lencioni, Patrick. *The Advantage: Why Organizational Health Trumps Everything Else in Business.* Jossey-Bass, 201Reflection #17

Lomenick, Brad. *H3 Leadership: Stay Hungry, Be Humble, Always Hustle.* Nelson Books, 201Reflection #39

Llopis, Glenn. "5 Things Failure Teaches You About Leadership." *Forbes*, August 20, 201https://www.forbes.com/sites/glennllopis/2012/08/20/5-things-failure-teaches-you-about-leadership/#efe9af168bbReflection #93

Loftus, Geoff. "The Greatest Leader of All." *Forbes*, April 2, 201https://www.forbes.com/sites/geoffloftus/2014/04/02/lead-like-jesus/#3baf18d963b9. Reflection #86

Marcos, Juan Carlos. *Warriors at the Helm: The Leaders Guide to Success in Business.* Elie Press, LLC., 201Reflection #33

Murphy, Shawn. "10 Tips for Creating an Optimistic Workplace." *Inc.*, January 26, 2016. https://www.inc.com/shawn-murphy/10-tips-for-creating-an-optimistic-workplace.html 2016. Reflection #91

Nepo, Mark. *Seven Thousand Ways to Listen: Staying Close to What Is Sacred.* Simon & Schuster, 201Reflection #55

O'Toole, James. *Leading Change: The Argument for Values-Based Leadership.* Ballentine Books, 1996. Reflection #68

Psychological safety definition. Simon Sinek, *Leaders Eat Last.* 2014, 2017. Reflection #78

Irving, Justin. "People, Planet, and Profit – Business Leaders and Sustainable Economics." *Purpose in Leadership*, July 25, 201https://purposeinleadership. com/2014/07/25/

people-planet-and-profit-business-leaders-and-sustainable-economics/.
Reflection #99

Rath, Tom. *Strengths Based Leadership: A Landmark Study of Great Leaders, Teams, and the Reasons Why We Follow.* Gallup Press, 2008. Reflection #90

Riggio, Ronald E. "The 4 Elements of Transformational Leaders." *Psychology Today,* November 15, 201https://www.psychologytoday.com/blog/cutting-edge-leadership/201411/the-4-elements-transformational-leaders. Reflection #89

Smith, Jacqueline. "10 Reasons Why Humor Is A Key To Success At Work" *Forbes,* May 3, 201www.forbes.com. Reflection #47

REFLECTION INDEX

ABOUT THE AUTHORS

Kelly Tomblin serves as a CEO in the energy industry and brings more than twenty-five years of diverse leadership experience as lawyer and business executive. Awarded Global CEO of the Year by S&L Platts as President & CEO of Jamaica Public Service, her unbridled energy, advocacy, and vision have distinguished her as one of the most dynamic and accomplished leaders in her industry. Throughout her career, she led companies and teams in a male dominated industry and found a way to drive a healthy culture that balanced masculine and feminine energies. In every role, she created platforms that facilitated time and space for mindful leadership that supported a fundamental shift in the interpretation and display of power. Both on and off the job, she is a passionate advocate for women and diversity, and is committed to discovering the genius in others and putting it to work in the world.

Tomblin has taught many teams the way to "do power differently" through activating true power. She is a speaker worldwide on organizational alignment, leadership, and gender equality. She founded the Jamaica's Women in Energy, an organization designed to uplift women and launched the JPS Foundation, a nonprofit organization supporting schools and nutrition. She is a former United Way Platinum Award recipient and she served as a Board member for Junior Achievement.

Tomblin has an MBA from New York University's Leonard Stern School of Business and a Juris Doctorate and BS in Journalism (with a public relations concentration) from West Virginia University. She currently resides in Chicago.

Kathleen Sullivan is a passionate catalyst for human and organizational potential. As a leadership and organizational development consultant she has over twenty-five years working in several industries across many cultures. Her corporate career has spanned managing call center, customer service, engineering and IT operations to leading global IT and HR support organizations. With a deep understanding of the interrelationships between people and operations, Sullivan uses that knowledge to help leaders create productive and healthy work environments. She has a fervent desire to bring compassion, humility and inclusion into the leadership conversation to create a new paradigm for power.

Sullivan has an MBA from Monmouth University and a BS in business administration from Georgian Court University. She is a certified leadership coach with the Coach Training Alliance and an Insights Discovery® practitioner. She is vice-chair of the Charleston/Low Country advisory board for the South Carolina Ovarian Cancer Foundation (SCOCF). She also served as a member of the board of trustees for Georgian Court University and the advisory board for the University of Idaho's Public Utility Executive Program.

Sullivan has been an avid photographer for many years and has always used her photography to access a deeper level of thinking. Through her "soul images," she seeks to provide a window into the beauty, inspiration, and grace that can easily live with us in the workplace. She maintains homes in Charleston, SC, and on the west coast of Ireland in Co. Clare.